Cross Currents

A Memoir

Wisdom
Editions

Minneapolis

Second Edition December 2022
Cross Currents. Copyright © 2022 by Rose Ann Findlen.
All rights reserved.

10 9 8 7 6 5 4 3 2
ISBN: 978-1-959770-50-3

Cover and book design by Gary Lindberg

Front Cover: *Bridge Trestle over a River*,
photograph by Rose Ann Findlen, 2015.

"About the Author" photograph by Mary Ellen Bates.

Back Cover: *The (Old) Amelia Earhart Bridge*, Atchison, Kansas, 2012. Photograph by Robert Elder. Used with permission.

Cross Currents

A Memoir

Rose Ann Findlen

Wisdom Editions

Minneapolis

For George and Sara

Contents

Also by Rose Ann Findlen

Missouri Star: The Life and Times of Martha Ann "Mattie" (Livingston) Lykins Bingham

Borderland Families Always on the Edge: Journey of the Lykins, Peery, and Heiskell Families along the Missouri Kansas Border

Waiting for the Fall: Short Stories

A Place in Northwest Missouri
September 2014

I cross into Missouri from the west this time, driving across the "Big Muddy" at Atchison, Kansas. I remember approaching this rusty iron bridge on a hot Sunday with my father in the 1950s.

"That river's dangerous," he said. "It looks calm on the surface, but it's full of holes you can't see, shifting sandbars and undercurrents. People drown in that river."

I had stared through the arches of the bridgework to see how dangerous the Big Muddy really was beneath its opaque brown surface. A few small pools circling the floating tree branches gave little sign of the treachery below. My father had said that undercurrents sometimes ensnared swimmers' legs, pulling them into the tangled mass of weeds. Though I couldn't see them now, I knew they were there, floating in water thickened with the soil of two centuries of the Borderland's blood hate and suppressed rage.

This afternoon the river has that same deceptive bland look. I cross the Missouri state line in the middle of the bridge. Here and there, a tobacco barn teeters before its final collapse. The river bluffs are behind me now, and rolling hills stretch out in front, lacerated with row upon row of dry cornstalks as if dug into the land by long fingernails. My grip on the steering wheel tightens. Whatever the road I choose for returning to Northwest Missouri, I dread returning to the confines of this place. At the same time, the smell of the rich black earth and the slant of light bathing the horizon draw me back.

When I reach the intersection of the highway heading north toward Iowa, I stop for gas.

"Sure is hot for September," the cashier remarks. "Supposed to rain, but the clouds don't much look like it."

"Are those tomatoes for sale?"

"Yeah. A guy brought them in this morning. They've canned all they want. These are probably the last ones for the year."

I hear the slow flat music in her voice. This is Northwest Missouri all right. I buy two big red tomatoes to eat on the road right away, knowing they're the most succulent tomatoes on earth. They are the taste of home. Whenever I come back to this part of the country, I feel a deep undertow pulling me there: hilltop trees silhouetting the horizon, the pick-up driver's hand raised in a short horizontal salute as we meet on the two-lane blacktop. A simultaneous push makes me want to turn the car around and drive away—away from the grimy plainness of the crumbling, deserted barns or their corrugated prefab replacements, the endless talk about the weather, and the drowning of who I am today.

I drive on to Maryville to meet them. This weekend my brothers' homes are filled with the families of their adult children returning for the reunion at my childhood home. I check into a motel at the edge of town. The sterile anonymity of the room underscores my sense of separation from this place where I lived, off and on, for thirty-four years.

In the morning, I drive to my brother Frank's country house to eat breakfast with the families staying there. As my white Nissan plows through the early morning fog, it may as well be a lunar vehicle traversing a crater on the moon. I turn my head to the left to look for a certain roadside marsh where red-winged blackbirds liked to rest on cattails and bask in the autumn sun. My daughter and I had sometimes waded into the bed of cattails in late summer to gather a fall bouquet. I roll down my windows so that I can hear locusts sawing their melancholy late summer song, but there is only the sound of the wind whipping through the open car window. The marsh is not there, having been drained to create a perfectly flat, rectangular field to accommodate the movement of the giant harvester that comes to scoop up the corn in a single day.

Nothing looks familiar. Where is the house where Weldon Townsend got on the school bus each morning? The house where my friend Joy and I perched on the porch roof plotting the next day's prank to play on her little brother?

I look toward the tree-lined fence row to see if deer are still grazing in the cool gray morning. There are no trees, no fence rows, no deer. Dry, barren cornstalks stretch from the edge of the highway to the horizon, silent and unmoving. When I had last driven this road five years ago, I mourned the abandoned farmhouses and giant red barns collapsing into themselves, forlorn emblems of the last breaths of farmers now buried in the Wilcox Cemetery across the section from my parents' farm. Now the ruined barns and houses are gone, along with their fences, windmills, chicken coops, lilac bushes and lovingly tended yellow irises. Under the maple trees holding each farmyard in their leafy embrace, a family had lived, staying up all night in the barn to birth a calf, walking down the roads to the one-room country school, or hoeing around baby green bean plants before the sun rose too high.

Instead of farmhouses dotting the roadsides, steel machine sheds squat gracelessly beside giant cornfields so that farmers driving to the corporate farmlands can access the farm implements which stalk across the fields, long-legged, metal-jawed insects gobbling the crop. With almost all the landmarks gone, I look hard to find the turn-off to my brother's house. Thirty years ago, he had sold his small farm and now, in his eighties, works as the trusted farm employee on an old friend's twelve-hundred-acre farm. When Frank doesn't drive the equipment himself, he sub-contracts a young neighbor to climb into the air-conditioned cab, earbuds in place, to tend the fields in the hours after his day job in town. Frank is the last farmer in our line, the last one who can repair his own tractor or look at the clouds and smell the air to predict the weather.

When I see the Sunset Memorial Gardens off to my right, I know I am near the turn-off to my brother's place. Driving there in his nineties, my father had "fallen asleep" at the wheel, having forgotten to inject himself with insulin that morning. His dirt-covered 1990 Chevy nosed into the stone pedestal holding up a sign announcing the cem-

3

etery's name. "Dad seemed to be driving off into the sunset to make a glorious entry into the place of the dead," my brother deadpanned. Frank is a master of the family's gallows humor. Instead of talking about our pain at seeing our father lose his strength and vigor, we chuckle, shaking our heads. Rather than express relief that Dad wasn't killed, we joke. Rather than face the loss of him that, in his age, he is driving toward, we laugh.

Across the flat, barren cemetery, bereft of landmark and memory, I see my brother's house. Five miles from our parents' farm, the wide-windowed ranch house is dug into a bank at the edge of the cemetery. Each morning as he loads the dishwasher, Frank looks out over the cemetery's blank expanse of grass studded with occasional faded plastic flowers drooping haphazardly in Styrofoam Grecian urns. Twelve-inch stone squares marking graves are conveniently embedded flush to the ground. The owners of the cemetery property take pleasure in how easily the riding lawn mower glides over the generations of the dead with no gravestones impeding its progress. Except for the stone pillars at the entrance, I wouldn't know there was a boundary separating the fields from the cemetery. The rows of corn flow over the brow of the hill like the river of forgetting into the blank expanse of cemetery grass. It's all just one big lawn to mow or harvest.

I had once asked Frank whether he planned to be buried there, in the cemetery outside his window, or in the cemetery where our parents lay within sight of their home place. He looked at me incredulously. How could I even imagine, after all the hogs and cows he has slaughtered, the deer, foxes, squirrels, and rabbits he has shot, and the injured animals he has lethally injected, that he thought his body had need for a resting place.

"Well, no," he said, dismissing the implied sentimentality of place and history. "I'm going to be cremated and flushed down the toilet."

I park the car on Frank's front lawn. He stands in the fog, a weathered gray piece of granite sticking up in the middle of the plaster statues of Snow White and the Seven Dwarves at the entrance to their dugout house. His wife put the dwarves there before I moved away the final time. My brother's tall, lean frame looks incongruous among the Disney dwarves as he stands assessing the dark bank of clouds massed, beyond the fog, on the horizon. His wife, a city girl, chooses to cover over the lawn with cuteness and sentiment, not missing anything that disappears. Frank remembers, but denies, his losses, pushing them stoically beneath the stream of everyday events.

"Everything looks so different. I could barely find my way out here. What has happened?" I ask.

"Ethanol."

He knows immediately what I mean.

"The cost of land has gone up so much that the farmers can't waste an inch. As the big landowners buy up the land, they are bull-dozing all the buildings, tearing out all the fences, cutting down all the trees and draining all the marshes. The fertilizers soaking into the soil and our drinking water are killing the streams, the fish and, probably, us. The wildlife is gone. The people are gone." He paused. "It's all gone."

One of my parents' granddaughters and her townie mid-management husband now own my parents' home place, my childhood home. They have made the sprawling old farmhouse into a spacious home complete with granite countertops and a Jacuzzi. Where I had swung from a rope swing on the scraggly old pine, a plaster cherub burbles at the top of a Grecian fountain. The giant hay barns have been razed, their broad walnut boards thrown in the ditch marking the property's edge. A greenhouse stands behind the house growing seedlings for the immaculately groomed landscape, obliterating signs of the old outhouse and chicken coop, which had been my place of exploration when I was a toddler.

Before arriving at the reunion for the noontime cookout, I school myself to make no mention of how the place used to look or how I miss it. The renovations and the loving care given the old farmhouse have saved it from the corporate farmer's bulldozer and, for that, I am grateful. The sound of the wind on the hill, the angle of the late afternoon light, and my five-year-old footprints still pressed into the back step remain. Our second year on this farm, my father put down a "back step," an eight by ten-foot rectangle of cement outside the back door. I have a deep kinesthetic memory of my ten-year-old brother Chad picking me up and planting my feet in the cold, grainy wet cement. He took a twig and wrote my name in the concrete by my footprints, "Rose Ann, October 1945."

That will have to do.

My brother watches me make small talk about our family's way of making deviled eggs (vinegar only, no mayonnaise) and hears me point out my father's rusty old threshing machine still guarding the neighbor's filled-in catfish pond across the road. We look at each other in a rare moment of understanding and shared grief, our connection to this land pulled up by the roots and flung into the roadside ditch.

I want to say to him that I know what he and I have lost, that we're the only ones there who remember the farm and landscape that are stamped into our deepest selves, shaping how we've faced our days. I look at him, preparing to try to say it to him.

"Well," his wife says to me, "I just got a new smartphone, and it takes the most wonderful pictures. Let me show you our new grand-baby." She wedges her body between Frank and me, squinting at the screen as she searches for Baby Brian. Frank slips away and, once again, our moment for coming closer together is lost.

I smile and coo over the baby pictures, forcing my attention to the smartphone and the deviled eggs. I am sad, but not surprised. The lost moment is an iteration of our family way of speaking—self-depre-cating humor, understatement, irony, bland surface comments floating above a tangle of unspoken hopes and resentments. It's not our way to directly state our thoughts and feelings, and, after all, I chose long ago to put myself outside the perimeters of this family and this land. Outsiders, above all, will not get below the surface.

Back in my motel room on the third floor, I pour a glass of mer-lot. How in the hell did I get out, I wonder. What part of this place, for better or worse, still lives in me wherever I go."

I watch a rain squall sweep across the cornfield outside the win-dow as it passes iridescently between the sunset on the western hori-zon and me. During the spring and summer in Northwest Missouri, we kept an eye on the clouds. My mother taught me that lowering dop-ple-bottomed clouds portended a tornado. We watched approaching swirls of charcoal-edged thunderheads to see if spouts would form. "It gets real still before a tornado strikes," she said. One ominously silent, heavy afternoon, we watched a little twister snaking across the pasture behind our house between the chicken coop and our garden. That night, we listened for the sound of a freight train passing overhead and, on hearing one, headed for the basement, having walked through a flattened, splintered small town nearby the Sunday before. The fabled pieces of straw driven into barn boards, refrigerators perched in trees, water sucked from cisterns, and children's teddy bears thrown indifferently to the ground ten miles away were not figments of our dreams or imaginations, but real.

As a little girl of five, I walked silently through the familiar town reduced to a pile of shattered stores and houses, holding my mother's hand and hearing birds twittering and ruffling their feathers under a bright Sunday morning sky. It was, perhaps, my first awareness of the sudden death and violence that unpredictably blotted out sun-filled days in this land.

In winter, we sometimes woke to look out on a farm landscape transformed into white lace telephone wires, silver-coated trees and snow flashing with sparkling light. On those magical, crystal days, the ice froze to death the lambs born too young, broke the tree limb that held my swing, and annihilated tender white pear blossoms just in bud.

I petted and cuddled baby chicks when they had arrived as fuzzy peeping babies at the post office in early spring. Six months later, I pulled out the scalded feathers of those same chickens, now beheaded and, only minutes before, flapping crazily on the grass.

On a summer day, our family dog lunged at my face after I accidentally kicked his crippled leg as we played together. Even though I told my father it was my fault and begged him not to, my father shot Nero the next day as "a mean dog." One day he was my play companion and the next day he was a mean dog shot dead. That was the way it was, I was told. Years later, I understood that I did not want to stay there, a land so achingly beautiful but so often marred by capriciousness and ugly contradiction.

Brothers

When I go out to Frank's house to say good-bye on the final morning of my visit, he motions me to come into the garage. He has cardboard boxes spread out on the floor.

"I got these books at garage sales. Some of them are pretty good. I thought you might like to take some of them back with you."

He's right. Some of them do look pretty good—David Mc-Cullough, Stephen Ambrose and other historians. Visits to Northwest Missouri always involve getting little gifts to put in the trunk and take back to wherever I'm going—jars of bread and butter pickles, clumps of lilies of the valley to transplant, family photos, an old-fashioned food grinder.

"Take whatever you want. I'm done with them."

I pick through the boxes, remembering that he has always read western novels and history books.

"Oh. Here are some old photos too. And I found some postcards that you sent the folks when you lived in New Mexico."

The brittle rubber band holding the postcards breaks in my hand, and I look through the little stack. There, on top, is Route 66—Central Avenue—as it was in 1970, the year I returned to Northwest Missouri from Albuquerque to come to terms with myself and the mess I had made of my life.

I drive away, glancing at the rearview mirror. My brother stands, thumbs hooked in the front pocket of his Levis, watching me go. He smiles a little, perhaps even looking a little affectionately and sadly in my direction—at his age and, having lost as many family members as he now has, he may be thinking that we'll never see each other again.

Then his eyes shift toward the yellow cornstalks in the field across the road, and he turns away, back to his day.

What a little girl crush I had on him when we were both growing up. How I wanted him to love—or, at least, *like*—me. But all of us were wrapped up in our own struggles to see ourselves and figure out how we were going to navigate a confusing post-war world outside the perimeters of our farm.

I was born in the spring of 1942, three months after the bombing of Pearl Harbor. My three older brothers were obvious targets for the draft that immediately followed. My oldest brother Marshall, drafted that winter, was given a deferment until his second semester of college was completed. In the midst of angst and turmoil over sending her firstborn off to war, my mother was about to give birth to me, her last born. The family doctor had, no doubt, taken note of my mother's age, forty, and of the nearly impassable muddy roads he would have to travel if she gave birth at home.

In Missouri, the month of March can be ugly and unpredictable, so for everyone's safety and convenience, I was the only child in the family to be born in a hospital. That marked me, from my first day of life, as fundamentally different from my brothers and sisters. They were members of a different generation, and how they negotiated male-female relationships characterized that difference.

As my brother waited for his induction at Fort Leavenworth that July, he carried me everywhere in the crook of his arm. As he paced the living room and held me by the stomach under his arm, I cooed and looked out at the world, oblivious to the maw he was staring into. Did he yet know about the Death March in Bataan that spring and foresee that he was going to be sent to the Philippines? Did he know that the unprepared US and its allies were losing the war in the Pacific and that his country also would be fighting in Europe by November?

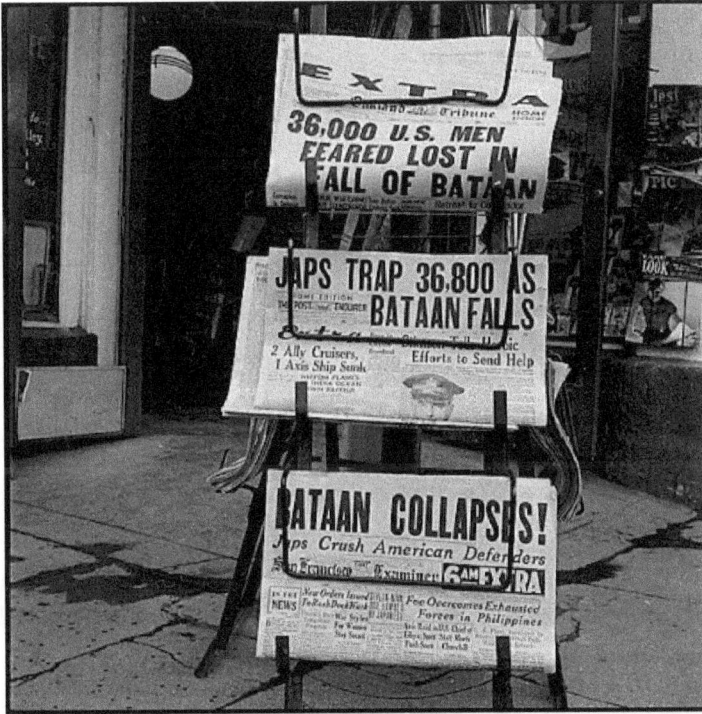

My role as Baby Rosie was to represent the normalcy of family and home and distract him from what awaited. We were closer then than we ever were after that. He liked me as a baby—not so much as a grown-up who refused to play by the rules of love and gender that he knew. He launched into his life as an adult just as I was launching into my first year of life. As I grew up, he was always more like a disapproving uncle than a brother. It grated on him that I was neither the little woman in the home nor like the meek dutiful women in his typing pool at the bank. Most of all, I was a threat to his role as "the family brain." He and I never knew, let alone understood, each other.

My father and his second son Rudy assumed the civilian duty of raising crops to supply the troops, Rudy's damaged heart preventing him from following Marshall into the jaws of the war. I was too young to understand what was happening when Rudy and my sisters' teenage friend joined hands and went upstairs together to bed. That was the moment my sister told my hurt, flabbergasted parents that Rudy and

Della had crossed the Missouri River to get married in Kansas and were going upstairs to spend their first night together as a married couple.

At that moment, Rudy crossed into the "Uncle" category at the age of eighteen. His first child was born by the end of the year, and it was she, not he, who was my playmate. Marshall, too, married his first girlfriend when he came back from the war. My two oldest brothers took my father's path in love: marry the first girlfriend, get busy making babies and then provide for them. That was my first impression of what men did when it came to love and marriage: procreation accompanied by responsibility.

My third brother was lost to me in another way. Mom wrote in her diary that during the war years, she "watered the garden with her tears." Max, a high school senior, saw the military as his ticket out of the farm life he hated and his conflicted relationship with my father. He could not fit the farm boy mold. My parents knew he would run away to sign up the moment he turned eighteen, so my father reluctantly agreed to drive him into town to enlist in the Air Force right after his birthday.

In the stoical way people handled their sorrow in Northwest Missouri, my parents didn't talk about the war or their fear in front of their children. But when the news came on the radio at 7:00 a.m. and 12:00 noon, my parents listened to every broadcast, trying to catch any bits about what General MacArthur was doing in the Philippines where Marshall was stationed. Occasionally a bundle of letters arrived from him which had words blacked out by some unknown third hand. Because of his own self-censoring hand and the additional assistance of the army censor, my parents did not know that Marshall was locked weaponless in General MacArthur's communication tower. His job was to send the General's top-secret communiqués.

As a ball turret gunner, Max was in much greater danger than Marshall. His slight frame and two machine guns were stuffed into the Plexiglas sphere suspended under the belly of the B-17 as he flew forty-four daytime missions over the English Channel and enemy territory.

The Death of the Ball Turret Gunner

From my mother's sleep, I fell into the State,
And I hunched in its belly till my wet fur froze.
Six miles from earth, loosed from its dream of life,
I woke to black flak and the nightmare fighters.
When I died, they washed me out of the turret with a hose.

Jarrell's note:

"A ball turret was a Plexiglas sphere set into the belly of
a B-17 or B-24, and inhabited by two .50 caliber machine
guns and one man, a short, small man. When this gunner tracked with his machine guns a fighter attacking the
bomber from below, he revolved with the turret; hunched
upside-down in his little sphere, he looked like the foe-
tus in the womb. The fighters, which attacked him, were
armed with cannon firing explosive shells. The hose was a
steam hose."
Randall Jarrell, 1945

When there were reports of planes shot down, my mother abruptly left the breakfast table and went to her garden to hoe. Two farms
away, their friends Lloyd and Edith Morgan also had a son in the war,
and when my parents were with them on Saturday nights, they talked
across the card table about the endless war.

My parents' second source of news came from war newsreels
designed to mobilize the citizenry and keep it working for the country's defense. As a farmer, Dad was allotted extra rations of gas, and so
we occasionally went to Maryville to the movies. The movie theater's
double feature format was to have newsreels followed by a "drama"
(meaning a war movie or a western), then a comedy or musical to
cheer us up. I didn't understand the meaning of war or of the bigger-
than-life Japanese Kamikaze pilots laughing maniacally as they tipped
their planes straight at me, machine guns blazing. I sank down into my
seat, unable to watch them. They terrified me, even though I did not

make the connection that somewhere in the South Pacific they might be shooting at my brother. My only notion of death at age three came from my realization that the baby rabbit I carried around all day one day was, as my mother explained, dead.

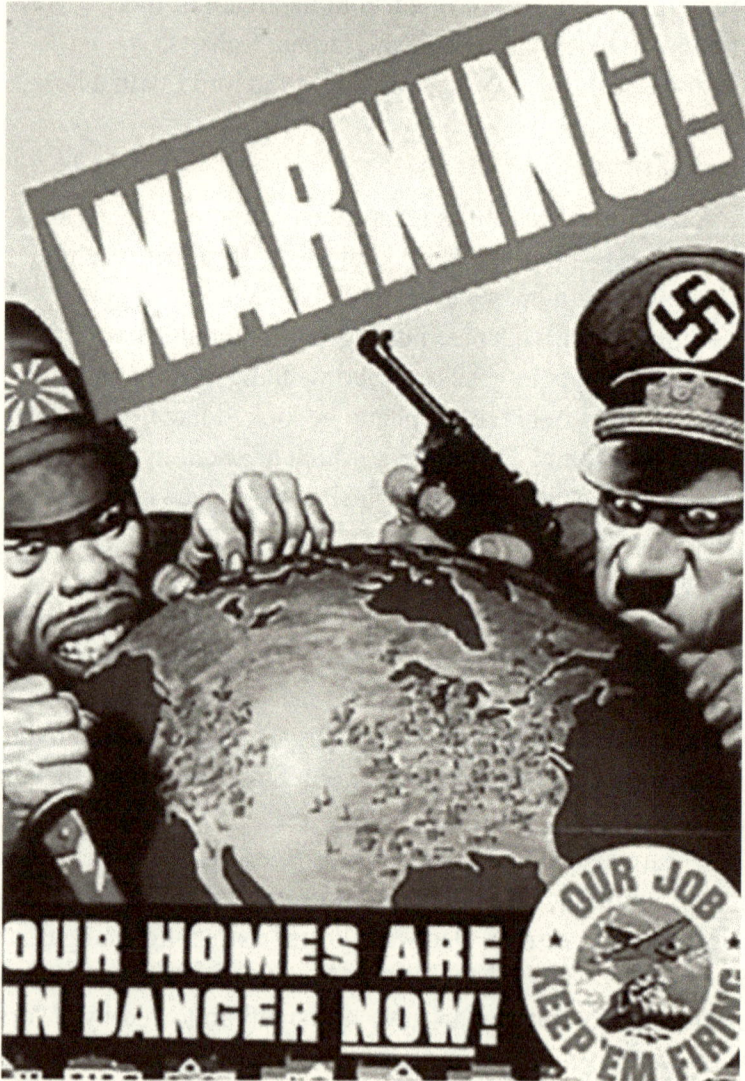

Warning our Homes Are in Danger Now! General Motors Corporation, 1942, NARA Still Picture Branch (NWDNS-44-PA-2314)

One Saturday night, when we got home from the double feature around midnight, it was raining. I heard talk of "being mudded out" and having to leave the car at the corner of the section and walk the half-mile home. I didn't like the idea of my bare feet squishing into the cold, wet dirt and still felt unsettled by those men with the machine guns I had just seen, so I pretended to be asleep, wanting to be carried home in my father's arms and to feel safe. That wasn't going to happen.

"Okay, Rosie," my mother said. "We know you're not asleep. Come on now. We have to walk home, and no one is going to carry you." We left the Hudson by the side of the road and walked into the black, still night, our feet making sucking sounds as we lifted them off the slick, rutted road. I was getting a first-hand lesson on the notion that sad or scared or not, "we just do it."

One night I woke up around midnight and saw our entire household gathered around a young man seated on a chair by the front door. Leaning against his knee was a big khaki duffle bag. Everyone was happy, talking to him in hushed voices. Max had gotten off the big 11:40 Trailways bus in Wilcox and hiked the mile home. The war was over, and he was discharged from the Air Force. He didn't talk much about his war experience. Instead, he chose to talk about his travels during military leaves in England, but the trauma was there.

Mom often told me, "Max won't eat mutton. One day I was cooking some for dinner, and he walked in and told me that he couldn't stand the smell of mutton and would never eat it again."

The smell of mutton brought back memories of himself as an eighteen-year-old kid eating Air Force meals in England laced with the terror of going on yet one more mission. My mother never served lamb again—not even after my GI bill brother moved to Arizona to get his master's degree.

Fifty-five years after the war, as Max fought the cancer that was killing him, I got to know him a little. He and I had never spent as much as two hours alone together, but as the cancer advanced, I went to California to be with him. We didn't know each other, but we were "blood." A cautious, private man, he circled around intimate topics when we drove on the freeway to his chemo sessions, never commenting on his distancing himself from Missouri and the family or of his choice to never marry. He had put a protective shell around his private life for so many years that he didn't know how to begin to talk.

I came to understand his war trauma and something of his first love as he lay dying. As his kidneys failed, he began to hallucinate and saw over and over again the moment when his best friend in the B-17 next to him was blown out of the sky.

"Poof. Poof. He was gone."

I was with Max the night he died. Before he sank into a final morphine-induced sleep, he said, in a last moment of clarity, "Rosie, I wish I could have done more for you."

Even in his absence, he influenced my life more than he knew. In rare moments stolen from the war, I first learned to love music, reading and the idea of travel on his lap. When Max came home on furlough, he pulled copies of music from our piano bench and hungrily played. The music bench was full of popular sheet music with garish pictures of Rita Hayworth and Betty Grable and stacks of dull, serious-looking yellow-covered books that said things like "Sonata in F" written on them. I first learned to sing songs at Max's side and to read books at his elbow.

He loved to intone the stories which he knew I had memorized long ago and insert new words and plot complications into the text as he read. I indignantly corrected him on both counts and when he said, without changing his tone of voice or breaking from the story's rhythm, "Turn the page," I turned the page immediately, thinking at age three that the words "Turn the page" were part of the story.

He encouraged my verbal antics. One day he asked me to get him a glass of "our good old hard water." I ran to the kitchen and came back flinging ice cubes, which he laughingly fended off, loving my acting out a pun. I think he knew, or perhaps hoped, then, that I, like him, was not meant to stay on the farm but to embrace some other storyline. The journey he made away from Missouri had connection points with my own, but we never got to talk about how I heard his voice and followed its call.

My relationship with these three older brothers was mostly characterized by their absence, their separateness. I saw Marshall a few times a year at family gatherings. If he spoke to me at all, he scorned and put down any opinion I offered. Rudy's only way of relating to children was to grab at them as they darted past and hold them captive. Max simply wasn't there, except in my head. Frank and Chad were teenagers at home when I was in grade school, and they followed Marshall and Rudy's treatment of my sisters and me, teasing, scorning, criticizing and ignoring. One February morning, I woke up early and tiptoed excitedly down the frigid, unheated staircase. I put a valentine in the center of each of my brothers' breakfast plates, eagerly waiting for them to smile at me and say, "Thank you, Rosie."

Frank, sullen and aloof, flung the valentine to the floor, my little girl heart with it. Why couldn't he just like me a little?

Remembering that morning, I feel the sting of that disregard. I know he must have been trying to find his own place in the family and in high school, where he locked himself into rebellious conflict with the teachers. That's forgiven and understood. He was a teenager. The little girl hurt from my brothers' absence and rejection dogged me across my own adolescence and beyond, but another part of me got mad. I would not bow to men who thought they could control me by putting me down. No.

My brother-in-law walked right into my need for affection and approval from men and my resentment of their unheeding sense of entitlement. On weekends, my oldest sister, her husband and three children often came to stay overnight. On one of those weekends, I got the idea of trying out a glamorous recipe I had seen in *Family Circle* to fulfill my unrecognized longing for male approval. I did not remember my male family members' suspicion of "different" foods and did not anticipate that I was opening myself up to relentless teasing. My parents permitted my brothers and other male family members to tease my sisters and me; the barrage of disparaging comments affected the self-esteem of my sisters and me more than my parents were able to realize, such "razzing" being a basic element of the culture in rural Missouri. My oldest sister absorbed the teasing and internalized the negative messages. My second oldest sister became a tomboy who could outrun and out-climb them all until she decided to stop running and stop climbing. And I fired back, unwilling to take the insults thrown my way.

Anticipating the praise that would reward my work, I labored all Saturday afternoon to create a Jeweled Pie for dessert that night. In my mind, I imagined the excitement when the family saw a pie pastry filled with a fluffy mound of Dream Whip and strawberry Jell-0 whipped together. Inside the pink mound of filling were the "jewels," carefully cut cubes of bright red, yellow and green Jell-0.

The moment my sister and brother-in-law came through the door, I led them into the kitchen to show off my creation.

"A Jell-0 pie?" my brother-in-law, Eldon, snickered.

"Yes! It is filled with red, yellow and green cubes that look like jewels."

"YUCK!" He walked away laughing.

He couldn't get the idea of the Jell-O pie out of his head and spent the afternoon commenting on how weird and ridiculous an idea it was. I began to seethe. The table in the dining room was stretched out to seat eight people that night. Eldon sat at one end beside my father, and I sat at the other end in what my mother called the "jump up seat," which was assigned to a daughter so she could get up from the table and bring whatever anyone needed. When it was time to serve dessert, Eldon couldn't stop himself from making one last snide remark about the pie.

No! My dammed-up rage broke out. I picked up the pie and pitched it across the length of the table and into his face. The Jell-0 hung like a long beard from Eldon's astounded face. Shocked into silence, everyone looked at my mother to see what would happen next.

Fortunately for me, my brother-in-law laughed. It was probably one of the most unexpected and exciting things that happened to him in his miserable, dull life. My mother's mouth gaped open as she tried to decide what to do about this flash of temper. As everyone began to laugh, she seemed to conclude, along with everyone else, that Eldon deserved what he got, and we moved on through the evening—without dessert. On one level, I think she saw herself in me, a brainy independent spirit not willing to be squashed.

The Riverboat Casino

A couple of miles from Frank's place is a T-junction. If I turn south, I bypass Maryville on the interstate and head toward St. Jo and Kansas City. That road goes to where three of my brothers lived—and died. If I turn left, I will drive North on Highway 71 into Iowa and turn toward the Mississippi River and points eastward. I turn north, my head filled with sights and sounds of my visit.

* * *

On my way to Maryville, I had stopped at St. Joe to meet my youngest brother, Chad, for lunch. Winding my way through the old down-and-out river town, I passed the sculpture of the Pony Express rider whipping his horse westward, which stood at the crossroads where stables of tough, sweating horses began their route. I made my way over potholed streets toward the stockyard, where thousands of cows began their final journeys to slaughterhouses back east. Before that, when riverboats commanded the river, the city's brick and white-trimmed mansions stood on the bluffs, their broad porches looking out toward the river and the promised land beyond. Now they were rundown, boarded up, scary-looking places to drive past, fluorescent graffiti threats and invitations dripping down their rotten sagging doors. No one going anywhere.

I looked for The Riverboat Casino, Chad's favorite lunch spot. My GPS was no help here. The bluffs looming above each side of the river blocked all signals. I finally spotted the casino, squatting gracelessly at the edge of the Muddy Missouri, blending with the river's dull, dirt-saturated waters.

Chad emerged from the dark, shaded depths of the casino. He led me through the labyrinthine hallways of the building. The lights of the gift shop's yellow sconces cast dull shadows against the gray walls, like the rotten-toothed leer of an old man, as we moved deeper inside toward the slot machines. Two sleepy workers slow-walked carts of food toward the steam tables in the cafeteria off to the right. I smelled the stale frying oil all the way from the kitchen to the entrance of the dining room.

Farther down the dim, silent hall, a mechanical musical ensemble cranked out "Swanee River." Invisible hands presumably belonging to the empty chair behind pressed the keys of the piano. The banjo strummed along, its player not in the chair but somewhere far away—maybe even in New York—pushing computer buttons.

"It's early yet. There'll be more people here closer to noon." Chad knew all the rhythms and patterns of the place. He was a regular. "Let's go hit a few slots while we wait."

"You'll have to show me what to do. I've never done this before." I squelch my lack of enthusiasm for the entertainment he's devised. He was trying to "show me a good time," and I needed to just do it. I got twenty dollars' worth of tokens, and we headed into the banks of idle slot machines.

"Hi, Gert—how's it going today?"

A white-haired woman swiveled on her stool, her feet stuffed into Easy Spirits, swollen and puffy as marshmallows. Her right hand rested on her thigh, a cigarette's smoke curling over light blue polyester pants. Her left hand hovered above a stack of tokens as she turned to see Chad.

"Well, not too bad. I'm $2.25 to the good. Haven't seen any jackpots yet today." She noticed me looking around vaguely for a place to sit.

"You're gonna be whistlin' Dixie if you set there. It's too close to the aisle. Find a spot that's behind a post or somethin'—not too convenient. Every slot has an allotment programmed for how much it can lose in a day. You want one that hasn't been tapped too often today."

She turned back to her slot machine, having said all she had to say. Her left hand dipped down to the tokens and up to the slot without a break. She moved into the rhythm of her game, oblivious.

"Whislin' Dixie!" I hadn't heard that one for a long time, maybe not since I left Missouri in the Sixties. The slot machines gulped down my tokens in about ten minutes, leaving me feeling emptied out.

My brother, always on the lookout for criticism, hastened to assure me that he was no profligate gambler. "I always come with a set amount that I'm going to play. And I stop at that. Over the years, I've come out about even, spending about as much in a night as I'd spend going out to dinner."

"I believe you," I said. "You're so tight you squeak. You aren't going to be pouring sand down a rat hole." Within an hour of crossing the border into Missouri, the family's way of speaking flowed effortlessly from my mouth.

I was no closer to Chad than I was to any other of my brothers, but, on some level, I understood him a little. I watched him pick at his prime rib and mashed potatoes.

"Do you feel all right?"

His skin matched the yellowish-gray light of the dimly lit dining room where we sat by windows overlooking the river.

"Well, no, I don't feel too good. I'm going to go back to my heart doctor next week. It seems like I can't breathe."

Later, as we stood beside his pick-up to get back on the road, he asked, almost casually, "Say, do you remember, are those cemetery plots up by the folks still fifty dollars? I'm thinking about buying three plots up there. My oldest boy and his wife want to be buried there too."

"Yes, they are still fifty dollars. Let me know how your doctor's appointment goes."

He hugged me, awkward and stiff, before he climbed up into his pick-up, lit a cigarette and drove away.

Now, sitting in my car at the T-junction, I can't forget this last image of him, gray and drawn as he hunched over his cigarette. I am filled with dread but am all too familiar with the unsaid, uncompleted ways we have said all we will ever say to each other. I turn north at the junction.

In six months, he will be dead, a squamous cell cancer having twined itself around his ribs, a poisonous vine reaching for his heart.

* * *

Heading into Iowa, I am still circling in a slow deep whirlpool of Missouri houses, brothers, the past and present, rolling hillsides of barren cornstalks and the casino. I remember the smell of the casino—dank, wet earth mingled with smells of deep-fat fried fish. It touches into a primal imprint, the smell of a damp dirt floor in the basement below Edith's kitchen. Glass jars of canned peaches, tomatoes and beans on the shelves gleamed dully in the darkness.

I was around five years old. Mom's social club, the Lone Star Women's Club, met monthly at the homes of the members. Mom and her friends talked for a while, played a party game to see who could list the most words beginning with "D" in five minutes, awarding the winner a hand-crocheted dishcloth, and concluded with coffee and a sweet. The children ran around the house playing tag and other games that everyone knew.

Edith Morgan was the hostess that day, so her thirteen- and four-teen-year-old sons were there, along with younger boys who had come with their mothers that day. Edith's boys were rowdy and coarse, but I didn't know that yet. The girls chased each other around and around Edith's house, playing tag. The boys were curiously absent.

As I rounded the corner of the house, boys' heads suddenly emerged from the cellar.

"We're playing cowboy down here," whispered one of the older boys. "Wouldn't you rather come down here and play with us?"

I stopped in my tracks, intrigued by their unexpected appearance and by their invitation to play—no boy had ever invited me to play before. My younger brothers, in fact, made every effort to avoid being seen with me. This all sounded more interesting than tag. I loved playing cowgirl, so I descended into the basement.

"Now we have to take you to the doctor," said the older boy. "Lie down on this table. Here, I'll lift you up there and take down your pants."

I was puzzled but willing to go along. I couldn't figure out why the younger boys were whispering and giggling in the background.

Without warning, Edith appeared at the cellar door. "That's enough of this," she said, remarkably calm. "Rose Ann, you pull up your panties and go on and play." She stood there until I reached my mother's side. I have never known how Edith knew I was down there or what they were planning to do—or if my mother ever knew of the event. I felt confused and frightened somehow, without understanding why. The coffee cups clinked on the glass snack plates, and the club meeting continued uninterrupted.

None of my brothers was in that basement, but the unsettling sexual menace of the situation entangled with their distance from me in time and space, our cryptic ways of communicating, our failure to connect. I interacted little with my brothers, either as a child or adult, but they deeply imprinted my notions of love, marriage, gender roles and, most of all, my identity. They were trees leaning precariously over the banks of the streams I waded in, slipping and sliding on wet rocks in search of love and acceptance.

The Facts of Life

I drive into Iowa in silence with no radio voices to distract me from hearing the distant voices of my father and brothers. Free associating the labyrinthine gray halls of The Riverboat Casino with my brother's lined face and my early life encounters with sexuality and danger is not really a stretch. As far back as I remember, it was those voices that taught me the little I knew about men and love. Whatever information or misinformation about sex I gleaned suggested threat or shame—danger.

Their words, in turn, resonated with what I learned at school. By day, the one-room country school a mile from our house was the place where I learned to read, said the "Pledge of Allegiance" each morning and played Andy-Over during recess. At night, during Community Meetings, the games took on another life. While parents sat inside discussing "Old Business" and "New Business," the boys organized into marauding bands lurking in the trees at the edge of the school grounds. They waited to catch girls making a desperate charge from the schoolhouse to the outdoor girls' privy thirty yards away. The girls formed a screaming mass running to and from the privy, some enjoying the rush of adrenalin, some allowing themselves to be caught and dragged off to the ditch to have their panties taken down. What occurred next I didn't know with certainty—rumors abounded among the throng of girls—I made damned sure I didn't get caught. I was terrified of being caught and held powerless against the ground by the gang of boys. When their feet pounded too close behind me or someone grabbed my sleeve, I ducked back into the school to sit at the edges of the room, hearing the "New Business" grind to a close. A gallon-sized speckled-enamel coffee pot boiled coffee in the background, and the scent of it brought the wild boys and girls back into the circle of light to inspect the rows of homemade pies.

My best friend Joy and I snagged the last pieces of gooseberry pie, taking them to sit on the long bench at the back of the room. Joy, a lively tomboyish girl, lived up to her name. Always laughing and darting across the playground, she easily out-ran every boy in the school and was in no danger of being caught in the nocturnal chases on Community Meeting night. If somehow she had been captured, she would have slugged her way out.

When school was out for the summer, our mothers occasionally arranged for Joy and me to get together for an afternoon. One hot July day, she and I tired of walking the rafters high up in our cattle barn and jumping down into the wagon of oats several feet below. Catching and cuddling the little kittens barely old enough to walk, we sprawled together across bales, looking out the high hay-mow door at the cows in the clover field beyond the cow lot.

"Do you know how babies are made?" Joy asked abruptly.

"No. How?"

"Just like cows. The Daddy sticks his thing in the Mommy."

"That's not right. My parents would never do a thing like that."

My parents could not be part of an activity my mother clearly thought was so disgusting. I remembered when my mother and I drove to the fields to pick up Dad for dinner. As always, she added the potatoes to the roast to cook and we headed out to the North Place. Dad had driven a piece of farm equipment up there early that morning and now needed a way to get back home for his noon meal. On this hot drowsy August day, the fields somnolent with the sounds of late summer crickets, we sat in the car waiting for him to drive his tractor from the field to the North Place. As I sat in the car with the doors open, my legs dangled over the side of the seat, I gazed at the cows in the pasture.

I noticed a big red bull propping his front legs up on the hind end of an indifferent Black Angus cow, which kept intently tearing grass with her teeth and chewing it empty-faced. The bull, conversely, was huffing and snorting, intensely engaged in his project. I saw his penis, huge and swollen, swinging heavily in its weight. The bull appeared to be trying to insert this grotesquely misshapen, unruly organ into the back end of the cow. I watched transfixed. Mom, seeing me stare at the bovine pair, snapped, "Stop looking at that, Rosie! You're not supposed to watch that." I unwillingly pulled my eyes away. What was she getting so mad about? Why shouldn't I watch? No, I told myself, Joy's explanation didn't make sense. How could you make a baby out of that?

"Well, it's true," Joy insisted, angry that I would not believe her. She jumped up and climbed to a high rafter, daring me to follow.

Reflecting on Joy's assertion, I remembered a basement encounter with boys and penises years earlier and struggled to put the events of that day into relationship with the cow and the bull. This topic was not one that I could raise with my mother, I sensed, because she and Dad both seemed to get upset over nakedness and penises. My mother even dressed in the closet, so that I would not catch a glimpse of her half-clothed.

I had seen my father without clothes a couple of times, but I got the idea right away that I was not to "look." Because all the bedrooms were full of doubled-up, growing brothers and sisters, my parents kept me in a crib in their room until I was almost six years old. One night, my parents were awakened by panicked chickens squawking in their coop. My father bounded out of bed, naked as a plucked chicken himself, got his shotgun out of the closet under the stairs and went out to confront the marauding fox. He shortly returned, having frightened off the fox. While my parents played cards with friends the following Saturday night, I told the story, concluding with "and all he had on was his shotgun and his shoes." As my father thought about what all else I may have witnessed in that bedroom and would report on, he decided it was time for me to move upstairs to room with Laura, my older sister Louise having recently married.

My father's attitude about nudity puzzled me when I was growing up. The same man who strode out to shoot a fox in the buff was the one who bellowed at me when I accidentally observed him crossing the kitchen naked from the laundry room to the bedroom after his Saturday night bath. He was the same man who lay naked in the yard on a hot night covered only by a blanket. (Our dog Nero was as confused by this sight as I was and tried to drag him away, blanket and all.) This same man sat at the lunch table in his bib overalls and nothing more, his bare white skin flashing in contrast to the unbuttoned sides of the denim and the scorched red of his bare arms.

Yet, he was horrified when, as teenagers, my sisters and I wore slacks and—God forbid—shorts. He swatted our rear ends as we walked past him, commenting on how unladylike we looked. Years later, the three of us confided to each other that as adults, we had to overcome a feeling of shame about our be-trousered derrieres, our father's Victorian attitudes toward female sexuality carried forward to us.

I think, too, Dad must have been "a rear-end man." Otherwise, his daughters' immodesty would not have been so glaringly apparent to him. My mother and I had looked out the window one simmering July morning, watching him drive his C-model Farmall and four-row cultivator across the dam of the farm pond which lay between our farm and the McGuire farm next to us. Yvonne McGuire, a middle-aged, buxom neighbor, bent over her garden, weeding. As he stared at her rounded expanse, he drove right off the dam and into the pond. There was no way he could hide this lapse of his roving eye—my mother could full well see him at the base of the hill attaching a log chain to the mired down scarlet tractor to pull it from the pond. At noon, when she asked him how the mishap occurred, he sheepishly admitted. "I was watching Yvonne weeding her garden, and suddenly I drove off into the pond." Whenever Mom reminded him of it, her eyes twinkling, he reddened and laughed in embarrassed acknowledgment, a hint that underneath his prudery, a lively libido stirred.

My father's mix of lustiness, duty and prudery must have created messages, silences and confusion for my brothers as much as they did for me. I don't know whether my youngest brother Chad ever dreamed of going to, much less living in, another country or even a different region of his own country. I did not know, until our last visit together, that he had wanted to go to college. He went from "Homecoming King" to "Father" a few months after his high school graduation. Like his sister before him, he got no encouragement or financial support for going to college. He took a job as grocery checker at the local Safeway and dated his high school sweetheart.

I must have been at school and missed the conversation at home that determined that he would be marrying this pretty eighteen-year-old, who was six months pregnant. Mom, Dad and I attended the little wedding ceremony in Skidmore, and at that time, it never occurred to me that the couple's lives were pushed inexorably into their unhappy marriage by a culture, which said "that's what you did" and by having no access to birth control pills, first legalized for married couples in 1965. The marriage lasted more than twenty years, producing five children in six years, several nervous breakdowns for Kay, and a thin, sad, over-worked brother, his faced lined beyond his years, crushed by obligation.

While Chad became a father and a husband, my country school friends and I discovered that our little school was closing and that, the next fall, we would go to school "in town" for junior high. The transition did not change our fundamental directions regarding our sexual destinies but more fully delineated them. We had a larger arena for exploring and defining our inclinations. Marty chose girls and fast cars as his area of specialty. He turned his taste for western shirts and pearl-buttoned shirts into his high school identity as a fast-driving, sexy, dangerous prospect for girls to run after. Janet marched steadfastly forward toward getting married as soon as she could to do what she truly loved—cleaning house.

Along with our year of establishing ourselves in the new school, Travis and I moved into the shoals of adolescent sexuality, not at all sure how to fit into the established sex and gender roles. My mother's "talk" with me about menstruation was so vague and awkward that I couldn't make heads or tails of it. The talk that day went into no further detail about "becoming a woman." The only person I could think of to explore this topic further was my old friend Joy. Joy had moved into town and attended the public school in Maryville. I began school at its rival, Horace Mann. Students from the two schools had little interaction, and Joy and I saw each other rarely. As I grappled with the complexity of having twenty other students in my grade (it had always been just Marty and me moving from grade to grade), I missed Joy's brash exuberance and her knowing take on the world. A couple of summers earlier, Joy came to my house for the weekend. To escape the tagging along of my nieces and nephews, we had gone to the cattle corral to walk the fences and jump off the loading chute. Across the field, we saw Marty McGuire and two of his friends swimming in the pond.

"Let's spy on them!" said Joy, squinting across the sunny field. "I wish we had binoculars."

"I can get my brother's," I whispered.

We sneaked into the house past the croquet players, porch swing occupants and visitors bent intently over their Pinochle cards. I got the binoculars Frank had brought back from the Korean War. Then, because it was hot out in the corral, we filled a half-gallon fruit jar with ice and cherry Kool-Aid, our favorite. Back in the corral, we resumed our mission. Marty and his friends were now running and jumping into the water, their shrunken penises bouncing in front of our binocular view. Delighted with our hideaway in a circle of weeds at the base of the corral, we gulped down Kool-Aid and exchanged the view that naked boys weren't much to see, even though Marty would croak if he knew what we were doing.

If there was ever anyone I would have wanted to ask about sex, I would have asked Joy. No use asking my mother—she either wouldn't talk or didn't know, embarrassing me for asking as I listened to her vague stumbling explanations.

Joy invited me to her basement house on the East Side a few times, but she seemed like a different person to me now—someone I envied for her reckless, rowdy ways, but someone who also frightened me in her abandon. The East Side of Maryville was "the tough side," where basements waited for the "someday" when the families would have the money to build alongside ancient, rounded aluminum trailer houses and shabby little houses built eighty years earlier. It was this side of town where many of the wild boys who smoked, drove cars fast, and made bad grades lived.

Joy wrestled outside with these boys past eleven at night. She demonstrated cartwheels and backbends for any who would watch her trim legs flying above her head or her big round breasts thrust skyward. The neighborhood boys cheered her on, enthralled by her exuberant sexuality. One Sunday afternoon, her new friends—all boys—were again there, while her parents hid themselves away in the bedroom for several hours—a strange way to spend an afternoon, I thought. Joy was wrapped up in the teasing electric physicality of the moment and forgot that I was there at all. I felt lost and frightened, wondering whether she was endangering herself in some way I didn't understand.

Now Joy wasn't around to talk to any longer, so I sneaked into the school library during lunch hour when no self-respecting class-mate would be caught dead there. A shelf at the back of the library had brochures explaining "the facts of life" in terms so discreet that I was unsure whether they represented either facts or life. Somehow these brochures were separate from the intensity I'd seen in the bull or the boys hiding out to capture girls on their race to the outhouse or on the hesitancy to talk about sex by adults I knew.

I sensed a mass of tangled weeds and floating debris lying beneath the flat, silent surface of what I could make out about sex and love. One spring evening that year confirmed my sense of danger and vulnerability. Mom and Dad dropped me off at Edith's house to keep Mary Beth com-pany. Mary Beth, a woman in her thirties, had a severe case of measles as a child and the extreme fever left her with the mental age of a child. My parents and hers were invited to a card party with neighbors, so my mother explained, "By staying with Mary Beth, you won't be dragged into a boring night of slouching in a chair waiting for the grown-ups to finally go home. And you'll be company for Mary Beth."

Although Mary Beth was five foot ten and weighed 250 pounds, she was a lonely child. She spent her days babysitting nieces and nephews, laboring with her mother to can hundreds of jars of beans and tomatoes, and cleaning up after her younger brothers, Charlie and Tony. We were an odd pair roaming around the Morgan farmhouse with nothing we could do together and nothing we could say. Mary Beth was a tall, squarely built young woman with a broad, pale freckled face offset by short, home-cut black hair fastened on the side with a child's barrette. I was a physically developed but naïve fourteen-year-old who had just spent her first year at the high school "in town."

I did not know that Charlie, her brother, was home from the Army. I still remembered him as the thirteen-year-old boy who invited me into the basement on that afternoon years earlier. The three of us leaned against a fence at dusk.

"Hey, Mary Beth," Charlie said suddenly, "Why don't you go to the house and make us some Kool-Aid?"

As Mary Beth lumbered toward the house, Charlie leaned toward me. "Do you remember the basement? We could go there again."

I took off after Mary Beth and stayed at her side for the remainder of that long, long evening as I watched Charlie sit on the faded chenille couch pretending to read. Mary Beth showed me the rows of tomatoes she'd helped her mother can that day and took me on a tour of their cold, sparse upstairs bedrooms. Charlie tried to send Mary Beth to the far reaches of the windy old farmhouse, hoping to get me alone. As she roamed the upstairs hall looking for something to entertain me, I stuck to her side, desperately wanting my parents' Pinochle party to end.

I never told my mother about that awful night because I didn't know the words to say, but she seemed to figure out what was going on because those times at Mary Beth's house abruptly ended.

A small, delicate overture from a classmate went a long way to offset my fear and disgust at Charlie's crude proposition. The school year at Horace Mann ended with a day of softball and racing freely in the woods ten miles outside town. At mid-afternoon, a group of eighth graders and I sprawled in the grass on a hillside overlooking the softball diamond, sensing the transition before us into high school. We were the bookish ones looking down on the games below. I stretched out on my side in my red pedal pushers, my waistline making a curvy outline against the sky. I was a cat lying in the sun, aware of Stephen Brien's eyes looking at me from under his long curling eyelashes. I liked his light blue eyes and basked before him. He suddenly leaned toward me, his finger lightly tracing the zipper on the side of my pedal pushers. "You've changed," he said, and, folding his arm across his eyes, he lay back again against the hillside.

I never saw Stephen after that day. His father was assigned to minister to another congregation across the state, I heard, and Stephen moved there to begin high school. For the first time, I felt an intense longing that must lie somewhere within the scope of sexuality, a warm, positive emotional connection to those "facts of life" people talked—or more often—didn't talk about.

To this point, my observations of sexual relationships had more often led me to see them as treacherous sandbars hiding in the river. My silver-voiced classmate Dolores was my first friend pulled so abruptly off-course. Freshman year, I always stood next to Dolores in Chorus, learning to match her soaring soprano tones. One afternoon in late October, she was simply gone, her curvaceous body and sparkling coloratura voice nowhere in sight or sound. She had been skipping out of school during lunch hour to meet with her new boyfriend—a college man!

"We saw them in the graveyard," a friend whispered to me one afternoon. "We followed them to the graveyard and saw Dolores's five can-cans flipped up over the back of the front seat!" By early November, pasty-faced Dolores, her red lipstick pushed on too brightly, invited us to her bridal shower.

"Johnnie's quitting college and working as a meat cutter at A&P," she chirped bravely. "We're getting married and moving to Clarinda."

"Can you get pregnant from kissing?" Connie asked me when I stayed at her house later that night.

"I don't think so," I said, combing my memory for references to that in the facts of life book.

"Well, I just want to be sure—I have a date with Willard Turnipseed on Saturday night."

"*Willard Turnipseed?* Is that a real name? Would you go anywhere with someone named Willard Turnipseed?"

"Yes, it is his real name. He may have a funny name, but he's nice. I met him at church."

We reviewed what we knew of the rules for dating. High school dating and sexuality had brutal laws determining our fates and dividing us into the initiated and the uninitiated, the ones who were driven and reckless, the ones who hung back dateless, or, like me, the ones who tried to walk the way between. The unwritten laws exacted payments from us all, their papers of indenture stamped with "Popularity" at the top of the page:

Popularity

1. Athletes and other popular high school men only go with girls who "put out" or make it seem like they're going to.

2. On a date, the girl must ask questions exclusively about him and his interests; if she plays a competitive game, let him win.

3. A girl must participate in foreplay enough on a date to get asked out again but not get pregnant; it is her responsibility to see that things don't go too far.

4. Men don't like brainy girls.

5. College is for getting the MRS Degree. Typing and home economics are good fallback skills.

6. A prudent girl doesn't kiss until after the third date, or men will think she's wild and tell all their friends.

As Dolores and Connie each stumbled their way toward their destinies, I waited, so wanting to be asked out but unwilling to pay the price that seemed to be exacted for our adolescent passions. As we all struggled with our sexualities and our destinies, Miss Jorgenson, our physical education teacher from Minnesota, introduced a six-week course on the facts of life for the freshman girls. She apparently hoped that knowing the facts would somehow prevent us from succumbing to the passionate desperation for love, acceptance and popularity governing backseats on dirt roads throughout the county.

272 *Facts of Life and Love*

may well be the kind that will go on through the years. There used to be a saying that fitted this nicely. It went, "Never marry a man until you have mered and wintered with him." More important than the seasons are the emotional climates that you weather together. When you have seen each other through all sorts of situations that have called forth a variety of feelings and you still love each other, it may well be the real thing. If you have experienced together a wide gamut of emotions—sympathy, anger, resentment, sorrow, fear, hatred, as well as love—so that you know deep down inside how each of you feels under these conditions, then you can be said to know your loved one enough to expect the relationship to endure.

Thus we see that there is no quick and easy trick for testing love that will work reliably. Young people will continue to pull daisy petals and cross out letters in each other's names, seek fortunetellers, read tea leaves, and play all the other games that are such fun. But when it comes down to deciding seriously whether we are really in love or not, we turn to more reliable evidences such as those we have been discussing.

Lasting love is too precious to confuse with any of its dazzling substitutes. That does not mean that we should avoid anything but the real thing. Far from it. But it does mean that when all the fooling around is over, and we want to settle down to a lifetime of loving someone with whom we can be deeply and truly in love forever, we should stop playing games and take the longer, surer tests.

CHAPTER 12

That Question of Petting

THERE has always been some form of love-making between the sexes before marriage. Grandma called it "spooning." Mother and father "pitched woo." Long before that, couples in cold New England "bundled" by courting under bed covers with a board between them. Practices very similar go on among young people today under the names of necking or petting.

273

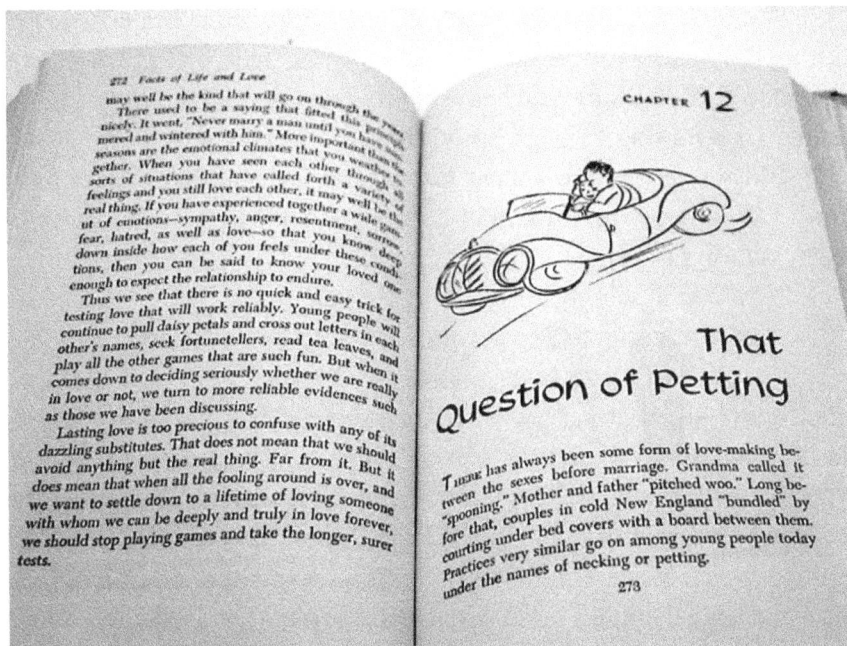

Dolores was already gone, but the other girls in my class toiled over notebooks in which we had to draw a penis and label its parts. Later we would have to pass a test for this course. Labeling the diagram was sure to be one of the questions—probably one worth twenty points, I thought, so I copied the diagram carefully into my notebook. Racing across the snow to the bus, I dropped the notebook, which, of course, fell open to the huge picture of the penis. I whipped the notebook up and closed, blushing at the idea of everyone seeing it face up in the snow. No one saw the drawing or recognized it as we all ran headlong to the buses to get seats by our friends and avoid having to sit by hecklers or nerds, the definition of who was which changing by the week. Miss Jorgenson's scientific approach helped us get the names of the parts right but offered no guidance on how to manage the sinkholes that came with them.

That winter, Miss Jorgenson asked me to stay after my physical education class.

"I have something I want you to see," she said, leading me to her office.

She took a hanger shrouded in long cloth from her coat hook. Lifting it up, she showed me a luminous white satin ball gown. It was weighted at the bottom with heavy double rows of cord covered in rose satin. "I was going through some things, and I thought of you. You sing solos at dances and appear in concerts. I would like you to have this." I wordlessly took the ball gown, overwhelmed by the sumptuousness of her offering.

"Are you moving?"

"Yes, I'm going to another job."

I had heard some boys saying something about "homosexual" when they talked about her. Having no idea what they were talking about, I stole into the library during lunch hour and tried to find the words in a "facts of life" book for junior high students. Nothing. The dictionary wasn't much help for "homosexuality"— Webster's Second defined it as a medical term for a "morbid sexual passion for one of the same sex." I couldn't make sense of it at all. Miss Jorgenson didn't seem sick to me.

The inexorable social laws governing our passions dealt with her, too, and I lost one of the best teachers I ever had. She and the school librarian, another woman, were fired overnight, apparently for being "too close." They moved to Denver, I heard.

The specter of pregnancy moved even closer to my life before the year was over. With unusual gravity, my mother met me at the door as I walked into the house after school.

"I have to tell you something," she said. "Frank is getting married to a girl from Kansas City. She is only a few months older than you, so you should get along just fine."

I frowned at her. What was this? Frank didn't even have a girlfriend. He never even went on dates. I remembered something about his going out with a waitress he'd met at my aunt's restaurant near Kansas City soon after he returned from Korea, but that had lasted only about three weeks.

"They are getting married on Wednesday and coming up here to live. You'll meet her on Saturday night at their apartment, and you'll be nice to her."

Why wouldn't I be nice?

I waited for Mom to say more.

"They're going to have a baby. Because Colleen is only sixteen years old and doesn't know anyone up here, she's going to need our help."

He was about to marry a teenager, big as a barn, who knew nothing of farm life, homemaking or the stoical ways of Nodaway County. Colleen's world revolved around riding around in a car, eating at fast-food drive-ins and talking about boys. They seemed about as incompatible as a couple could be but married they would be in two days. Frank, like his younger brother, was about to marry and become a father and, like Chad, he was going to have to find a way to make a life to accommodate those facts.

The need to be popular and desired ramped up my friends' overcharged hormone levels even higher. Cindy Lewis had dated a star basketball player for two years. When his high school stardom ended at graduation, he took a factory job in Kansas City. In her last year of high school, Cindy faced her friends' inquiring looks as her belly grew ever bigger and staunchly denied she was pregnant to anyone who dared to ask. By April, she married her basketball star. The high school principal stiffened his back and permitted her to finish the school year and walk across the stage to graduate, rare decisions in those times.

My best friend, Ginny, quit school during her first semester of college after discovering that her unrequited love for a local filling station attendant had left her on her own with a baby coming in four months. She went to the Home for Wayward Girls in Kansas City, gave up her baby for adoption, quickly married someone from the city and never returned.

Two of my schoolmates were notoriously promiscuous. Separated in age by two years, they barely knew each other, yet their sexual destinies tied them together in their future lives. Stacy Martin smoked, drove with a succession of men in speeding cars, and had sex with all or most of them (or so we heard). As soon as she squeaked through high school, she enlisted in the Women's Army Corps, where she continued the same pattern until she married another soldier, quit the army as married women were required to do, and rapidly bore three sons. By the age of twenty-six, she had died of cancer, and the boys' father was nowhere to be found.

The other, Audrey, my slender, quick-moving classmate, always made me think of a deer as she darted from one spot to another, her brown eyes taking in all details. She had two passions—men and journalism. As soon as she could drive, she dragged up and down the main street from the Dairy Queen on the south end to Franklin Park on the north. The status-conscious, cautious boys in my high school never really dated Audrey, but many were willing to go to a dark country road with her in her Buick. Young men who had already graduated and worked around the town were also quick to make Audrey's acquaintance and seek her favors. One night, having just gotten off being grounded for two weeks, Audrey put over one hundred miles on the Buick. She went to the eager filling station attendant, the one Ginny was in love with, and persuaded him to put the Buick up on the car ramp and run it in reverse until it had the mileage equal to the distance to a girlfriend's house. More than once, Audrey made trips to Clarinda, Iowa, thirty miles from the Missouri border. I never knew for sure what took her to Clarinda, but it was reportedly a place where a desperate woman could get an abortion.

In the years to follow, Audrey dropped out of college, continued restless, brief encounters with men and then married the last person any of us could imagine, an effeminate, obsequious funeral director. Marvin and Audrey couldn't have children, Stacy's mother explained to Mom, so they adopted Stacy's three boys. The boys, who had never recovered from the early loss of their own mother, were rowdier than Stacy's mother could manage. The three boys found themselves plunked into a sprawling house divided into living quarters and funeral home. The boys spent a few traumatic years hearing sounds of grief, embalmment, and Marvin's hushed funeral parlor voice beyond their living room door. Audrey, their adoptive mother, sought refuge at the country club. The wild, unhappy boys put unbearable pressure on the marriage, and Stacy's boys were driven in Audrey's expensive new Buick to foster homes, the struggles of Stacy and Audrey continuing tragically on through the lives of the three boys.

I watched my classmates struggle as the dual pressures of desire and role expectations set in motion their individual destinies, and I recognized my own vulnerability. The primary peril was getting pregnant, but blindly wading into an early marriage also scared me. By the end of our high school years, these two possibilities held greater sway over our futures than academic achievement, popularity or our individual aspirations.

By my junior year, I had met Jake. I was not attracted to him but hated seeing myself as a loser in the game of romance. As involved as I was in school activities and serious study, I loathed standing on the sidelines of school dances waiting for attention. I felt like a failure "as a woman," and I needed to prove that I could attract a man's attention and affection. I wanted to be seen as fitting into the presumed norms of high school culture. What I had not experienced, but longed for, were romantic love and male physical affection. Jake was available.

"You're dating Jake?" a friend asked me incredulously.

"Do you think he's smart enough for you?" my brother asked.

I felt sad and shamed by their questions because their doubts were my own. He was not at all gifted in school, and I certainly could not picture myself sitting demurely in a church pew as a minister's wife, but he was a good match for me within the inexorable dating rules by which we all tried to live. He was hotly attracted to me, yet his Christianity instructed him to stop short of sex. Our girded passions were all we shared, but in adolescence, that was all that mattered.

When Jake flunked out of college and joined the Navy, our relationship continued another year, but there was no energy in it. He gave up his dream of becoming a minister, settling for driving a 7-UP delivery truck in Kansas City after his Navy stint. I was relieved. I went to college, wrote poetry, sang and looked for a man who could love the me I wanted to become.

The Creek Flowing to the Mississippi
and Beyond

On this trip out of Maryville, I will drive all the way across Iowa, heading east toward the Mississippi River. Highway 2 goes along southern Iowa, not far above the Missouri line. The landscape still looks like Missouri, a plain once swathed in hardwood forests across its rolling hills. I take care to set the speed control at precisely 55 miles an hour, knowing that somewhere along this stretch of highway, a patrolman will be hiding behind a bush or just over a hill. The patrolmen enforcing speed limits on this deserted two-lane highway bring important revenue to the state as they snag impatient motorists cruising across the hills for somewhere else—anywhere else. People living in the area enjoy knowing that out-of-state drivers, driving as if they were on an interstate, will get their comeuppance.

I am not in a hurry today. The radio stations in Des Moines cannot reach between the hills on either side of the highway, and I relish the complete silence as the Nissan glides over the empty highway. I am at home with silence, having grown up listening through the quiet to coyotes howling in distant fence rows or cicadas chirping in the pine tree branches outside my bedroom window. Off to my left, a dead oak tree stands on a south-facing slope behind the rubble of a collapsed farmhouse. There will be morels under that tree next spring, some of the first of the season. Slowly I begin to relax. The voices of my brothers and father trying to define me recede, and another voice, spirited, imaginative and warm, emerges.

I am five years old again, walking along the little creek in the back timber with my mother. In my memory, we walk along the bank, my mother pointing out gooseberry bushes that we'll pick clean later, lavender Sweet William flowers in a spot of sun, luminous white May apple blooms hiding under canopies of sumptuous green leaves, and places where morels might grow.

"Morel season is mostly over when you see the May apples. Did you see the moss on the north side of that tree? Ethel says that means we're going to have a dry, hot summer, but I don't know if I'd believe that. She's superstitious. She also always plants her potatoes on St. Patrick's Day, but that doesn't make her crop any better. Makes more sense to plant when it's warmer, so you don't have to plant again if it's a cold spring."

"Where does that little creek go?"

She points to the small ripples moving south.

"This little bit of water, and hundreds like it, go to join bigger streams and rivers and together, they make their way to the mighty Missouri. The Missouri runs through St. Jo and Kansas City then turns east to the Mississippi. From there, it gets bigger and bigger. By the time it reaches New Orleans, it is a mile wide, flowing strongly to reach the ocean."

I had never seen any of those places she named, nor had I seen the ocean, but I needed to go there right away. It was my mother's voice that tied me to this land. She taught me to see the beauty in it, to savor the language and the stories, to work with its bounty. Paradoxically, it was also her voice that fired my imagination to leave as her stories flowed into my head.

Mom and I formed a close communion of two, passing the seasons together, as my sisters and older brothers moved on to begin their adult lives, and my two youngest brothers were off with Dad, at school, or with friends. Some summer mornings, Mom and I walked up and down the road, gathering dandelion greens to serve sprinkled with vinegar for lunch. When the gooseberries reached their full round maturity, we headed to the timber to pick buckets of them, rubbing them across a frame of window screen to remove the stems. As we foraged along roadsides or in the woods, Mom pointed to plants, naming them: chicory, cockleburs, wild roses. When the leaves had fallen in October, we raked them into giant golden piles which I plunged into, burying myself to sleep like Snow White.

In the long winter months, Mom must have grown weary of my constant presence on the floor beside her as she bent over the sewing machine making dresses for me and my niece Kathy. She bundled me up in leggings and coat and thrust me out the door "to blow the stink off." I pouted outside the front door for a few minutes, then forgot my resentment at being pulled away from building towers of dominoes or leaving my fantasy game in the tent I had made by draping a quilt over the card table. I soon pulled my sled through the snow, a female version of Sergeant Preston in the Klondike.

Other than our cats and dogs, I didn't have playmates until I was in first grade. My parents' friends had older children or none at all, and there were no little girls up and down our road. Marty McGuire lived on the farm next to us, but none of the parents would ever have dreamed of having me play with a little boy on a regular basis. My younger brothers certainly didn't want to play with me. They saw me, at best, as an annoying little sister trying to tag around with them and, at worst, as a threat, my having taken over their places as the baby of the family and robbing them of the scant special times they could eke out with my parents. Though their rejection stung me, I don't remember being lonely at that age; my day was filled with interactions with adults and imaginary play. I was comfortable with "entertaining myself," as my mother put it, and being alone with pets, my Little Golden books and crayons, the rope swing in the front yard, and the cloud-studded sky.

As children of older parents often do, I watched the adults and listened to their conversations. I became an observer. On visits to neighbors and relatives, I had glimpses of houses and ways—poorer, more old-fashioned—different from ours. Three farms west of us, the Leakeys had kerosene lamps in their house long after we had "gone electric," and when Mom, Dad and I went there at night, the four adults leaned into their card game with a lamp centered on the big square dining room table.

Grace the Quilter kept flamboyantly plumed Rhode Island Red chickens in her yard. My mother would never allow chickens in the yard and persisted until Dad built a tall fence around the chicken coop to keep them, their droppings, and the resulting flies and smells away from the kitchen door. Also, at our house, we had white chickens, which laid the town-preferred white eggs. When Mom and I took patchwork quilt tops to Grace for quilting, we had to tiptoe gingerly across the packed dirt and chicken droppings to get to her house. Grace called off her yapping, tail-wagging white and black speckled hounds as we approached the inner circle of the yard near her back porch. Once inside, we sat close to Grace as she rocked and delicately stitched at snow-white quilt backs. She never allowed them to touch the dusty broad-planked hardwood floor punctuated with tin can lids nailed over holes to keep the rats out.

On the ride there, Mom had instructed me not to comment on anything I saw. I was to keep my mouth shut—good advice for encountering strange events and people in life, I later found out. Even today, I reservedly watch people around me to see what they are going to do or say and keep my own counsel—still the solitary little girl who didn't learn how to make friends in those years and who had to painfully discover how the world worked outside the confines of the farm community.

My mother worried that I did not have enough contact with children my age and realized that I was more than ready to read. Her attempt to get me to begin school in 1947 at five and a half had failed because a child in Missouri had to be six by the first of October, five months before my sixth birthday.

I waited impatiently. The following August, we began to gather up pencil boxes, crayons, a Red Chief tablet, paste and scissors with rounded ends. I stroked the red front of the tablet gently, delighting in the pad of lined pages underneath, sniffed the school paste over and over, and studied each color in the crayon box. I longed to use them and to learn to read.

For me, Wilcox represented my first step alone into a bigger world. A very big deal. The center of community life in 1948 was the town of Wilcox, with a church, a post office, a one-room country school, two filling stations and a general store. A bus going from Omaha to Kansas City stopped there at one of the filling stations three times a day to take on and let off passengers. The Depression years had vanquished the bank, the auto repair service, the farm produce and weigh station. Each day that summer before school started, I walked to Wilcox with Mom, counting the days until Marty and I could walk by ourselves to the school that was just around the corner from the post office.

"Every little girl should have a new dress on the first day of school," my mother declared. She began to sew a blue dress for her red-haired girl. The pink and blue plaid yoke with a matching ruffle around the skirt to trim the solid blue dress was an especially elegant touch. To get ready for my school debut, I cut my bangs with my new school scissors, creating a jagged, crooked line of red hair across my forehead.

"It will be hot at school at first," she said, "so you'll wear your red sandals, and we'll buy new winter shoes later on," not knowing that on a day in September, a ring of girls would stand in a circle around me, the fifth-grade ringleader, Stacy Martin, disdainfully pointing at my sandals. She and her friends, all older girls, modeled their brown and white saddle oxfords, new for the school year. They considered themselves the knowing ones, having the power to shame—and educate—the lone first-grade girl.

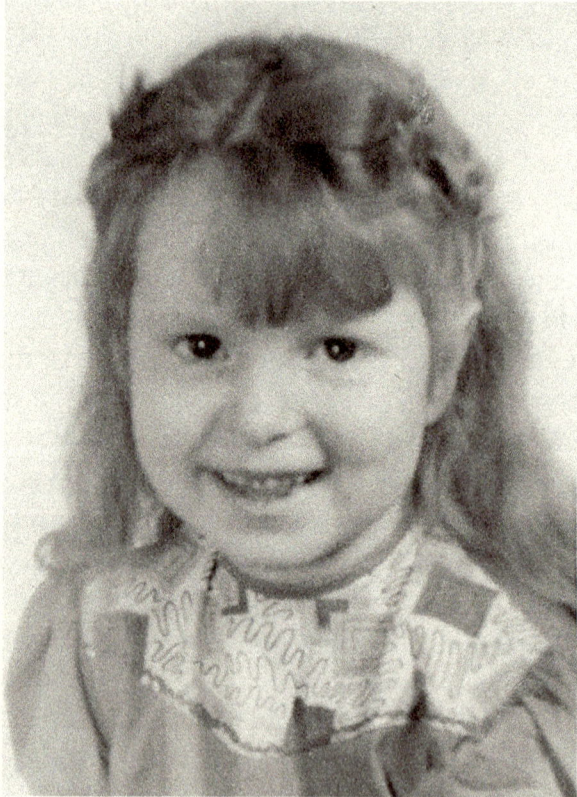

A second disappointment on the first day of school was that my teacher had not, as I'd envisioned, flipped on a switch in my head to instantly give me the ability to read.

"How was school?" Mom asked as I strode indignantly through the front door the afternoon of the first day.

"She didn't teach me how to read!" And so, my life at the one-room school in Wilcox began.

On Lord's Acre Day, the Wilcox Methodist Church's major fundraising event, all my classmates and their parents, believers or not, participated. My mother not being a "joiner" and my father not being a "believer" did not exempt them from contributing both time and money. The day before the event, our teacher canceled classes so that we could decorate a tractor-drawn hay wagon, stuffing squares of white and gold tissue paper into the chicken wire nailed around the edges of the wagon. During the parade, Marty and I starred in the tableau as Mr. and Mrs. Tom Thumb. The two of us, already assumed by many to be destined to marry, stood at the center of the hayrack—the "float"—along with the remaining student gotten up as members of the "Mr. and Mrs. Tom Thumb Wedding Party" or riding streamer-decorated bikes along the town's dirt road. My mother had strung some old fake pearls on a clothes hanger wire and bent the wire to hold my bridal veil, festooned with the pearls in front and a cascade of cheesecloth streaming down the back over my white wedding gown made from an old bedsheet. My six-year-old classmate Marty, another child of nonbelievers, dressed in a tuxedo (borrowed from someone who had been a ring-bearer in a fancy wedding). Though my parents were stubbornly skeptical and independent and his parents "wild"—known to go to dances on Saturday night and drink beer—we were part of the community. Marty and I were getting a formal introduction to our presumed future roles.

I loved the pageantry. For me, going to school in the little town of Wilcox represented excitement, change, and people to fill the space left by my departing brothers and sisters. I reveled in the excitement and novelty of preparing for all-school programs. Giggling and loud whispering children massed behind the big oilskin curtain, which unrolled from the school ceiling to reveal painted scenes and advertisements of local businesses. My mother had stitched together long drapes of brown cotton print fabric, which the big kids strung from wires to form the backstage and side stages of our makeshift theater. For two or three weeks, we formed small groups to practice skits interspersed with "pieces"—poems and monologues. Each of us, first grade through eighth grade, had to individually perform in front of the dropped curtain while scenes and costumes changed noisily behind us. The teacher stood behind the curtain, prompt book in hand, to help tongue-tied performers recite faltering poems and stumble through their pieces. Children performed pieces ranging from "Chopsticks" to "Moonlight Bay" on the decrepit piano and sang solos. Acting and singing came naturally for me, and I basked in both the challenge of performing and the compliments that followed when I sang "When Irish Eyes Are Smiling," "The Doggie in the Window" and "A Bicycle Built for Two."

I was lucky to have a good teacher that first year—my friend Travis's entry into the first grade the following year brought him terror. Teachers for the little school were scarce in those years and so, when my first-year teacher moved away, Todd Matthews, a lanky twenty-year-old man who'd completed—actually, probably failed—a year of college came on board. He was lazy and immature. Within weeks, the children began to get out of hand. As the long days of confinement with twenty rambunctious children closed in on him, a sadistic streak emerged. Todd's punishments for misbehavior included making a big chunky eighth-grader stand in the middle of the room, his arms outstretched sideways, holding a bucket of coal in each hand until he broke into a sweat. Travis, a year younger than me, couldn't "get" a math problem; Todd threw a kickball into Travis's stomach so hard it knocked him breathless and made him cry as he kneeled, doubled over at the blackboard. My father heard what happened to Travis and, as a member of the three-person school board, saw to it that Todd immediately left.

His replacement, a dull-witted fat woman of twenty-two with a year of college, finished out the year. She sat at the teacher's desk, her huge bare thighs plastered together under her tight cotton print dress, her round brown bovine eyes staring suspiciously at us.

"Do page 23 of the workbook, then pages 31–37..."

We were more interested in trying to see her underpants than we were in her plodding, unimaginative lessons. From second grade on, my education involved finding ways to occupy my mind. My school day was filled with opportunities to read on my own, invent projects and furtively daydream. One winter during grade school, I wearied of the mustard or sugar-and-butter sandwiches Mom sent with me for lunch. I had read all the books in the school, re-arranged the bookshelves to pass the time while other grades met with the teacher and watched the sweet potatoes sprout in fruit jars filled with red cake coloring-dyed water. As I sat at my school desk, I saw the hot plate sitting idle in the corner of the one-room country school. I hatched the idea that each student could take turns bringing cans of Campbell's soup to heat for everyone to have for lunch. The next week I brought enough cans of soup for everyone in the school, relishing the opportunity to escape from my desk to open and heat the soup. Soon other children took their turns, proud of the soup they had chosen for the day and their mothers' cookies and, in that way, organized their own hot lunch school program.

My turn to bring the soup came around again on Valentine's Day. Mom was not as busy as she once had been when all her children were in the home, so she made individual heart-shaped cupcakes for each child. I served the cupcakes mid-afternoon when we all took a break to exchange the valentines we'd brought to stuff into the decorated shoeboxes we'd made in art class. The students' eyes glowed when they saw the snow-white cakes lavishly covered with glossy peaks of divinity frosting and shredded coconut topped with a maraschino cherry. Mom sent along paper doilies to go underneath each little heart cake. This was the fanciest dessert many of them had ever seen.

Both at home and school, I invented activities for my hands and mind, always on the lookout for ways to enlarge my social and intellectual world. My parents' closest friends had no children my age, so when they played cards with them every Saturday night, I was required to tag along because my parents did not think I should stay alone until midnight in the big dark farmhouse. To entertain myself while they played cards—sometimes I joined them in playing five-handed pitch—I brought books from the library. Soon I was given the task of making the coffee and serving the dessert—Mom's strategy for shutting down my nagging to go home.

I dealt with being the only child in my parents' circle of friends and the only girl in my grade by taking on projects. In my last year at Wilcox School, the old games could not contain the energies of us older students—Janet, the lone eighth-grader, Marty and me in the seventh grade, and Travis, the only student in the grade below. We had outgrown our childhoods and chafed against our school routines as the end of the year approached. We stood peering into the black coal house no longer in use because of a new oil stove inside the school. The coal house was stacked high with discarded furniture, broken chairs, rakes, coal and bottles. Travis and I decided to clear this building out, clean it and make it into a play store. We persuaded the teacher that it would be a good educational project because we bigger kids would have to manage the old shed's renovation, decide what the store should stock and arrange to give the little kids practice with buying, selling, calculating change and amounts.

When Travis and I began clearing the building, we plunged into the project alone. We went home from school each day blackened with coal dust and exhausted from lifting and heaving the junk. Soon other children wanted to help—the little school population of ten or twelve children was soon feverishly waiting for recess each day so that the creation of the store could continue. Even Marty got involved, driving a tractor and wagon to school for us to load up with junk and coal to haul away. Janet and Travis's mother gave us leftover wallpaper, which we cut, measured, matched and applied. Everyone was so intensely engaged that recesses got longer and longer, the teacher unable to make us break away from the project. We finished the conversion of the coal shed to a play store that spring with still a few days before summer for the younger children to act out the roles of storekeeper and customer.

The freedom from regimentation worked for me. I occupied myself with teaching younger children, cooking up projects and reading. Before we got the oil furnace, I kept the schoolroom warm by stoking the giant coal furnace with chunks of coal between chapters. The arrangement worked for both the teacher and me. I brought extra books from the public library in town and stayed out of mischief. The teacher didn't have to stoke the fire between classes. I was like the tangled sturdy tomatoes growing in wild profusion in Mom's garden. My parents never pruned or staked their tomatoes, and the four dozen vines they planted flourished in the dark rich Missouri soil and soon were an entangled mass of strong green vines. Round succulent yellow and red tomatoes grew hidden among the leaves, unexpectedly robust and full in their offhandedly cultivated space.

During the long summer vacations, I ran out of ideas for amusing myself toward the end of the season. One afternoon in August, I sat spinning idly around in the rope and board swing hanging from the ancient pine tree in the front yard. The droning of the locusts, the chirping of the grasshoppers, and the dry brown grass beneath my feet punctuated the hot August silence. Staring at my bare feet as I dug my toes into the dry dust of the patch worn by hours of swinging, I was dimly aware of the tractor's drone in the field across the road. I was bored and lonely but didn't even know that I could feel otherwise on this afternoon at the end of summer. My isolation as the last child still on the farm was a fact of my life—the joys, the freedom and creativity of it as well as the loneliness.

Then there was a reprieve from my lassitude and unrecognized loneliness. The man on the tractor returned to his pick-up parked across the road. He stood by the open truck door looking at me in the swing, then strode across the road to our house. A minute later, he returned with my mother.

"Burt wants you to come home with him to stay all night and play with Joy," Mom said. "Do you want to do that?"

I was already gone, bounding up the stairs to stuff my shorts and pajamas in a bag. That night Joy and I squatted on the roof outside Joy's bedroom window, sipping Coke from a bottle and whispering together how we would convince Joy's little brother that he laid an egg in his potty chair. I would put him on the chair and tell him to cluck and pump his little arms up and down. Joy would be hiding behind a curtain next to the potty chair and slip a brown egg into the potty. We whispered and giggled until two in the morning when her parents finally said they'd been kept awake long enough. Our execution of the egg-laying plot worked flawlessly. Five-year-old Randy soon strutted through the house, cackling and proclaiming that he'd laid an egg.

For days after playing with Joy, I soared exuberantly through the air, re-discovering my pleasure in practicing trapeze moves as I re-membered that glorious twenty-four-hour reprieve.

Usually, my summer playmates were my older nieces and neph-ews, who appeared from time to time unannounced. Neither my adult brothers and sisters nor my parents made any special effort to pro-vide playtimes. They regarded end-of-summer boredom, like droughts and hail, as occasional random events to be endured as they occurred. Friendships just happened; they were not planned or sought—play-mates at recess in the winter and family members on Sundays in the summer. The people in your lives were just there, usually for life.

That predictability was about to change. On average, about twen-ty children attended the school in Wilcox, with no more than three in any of the eight grades when I attended. There had been more students when my brothers were at the school, but as the community members aged, there were fewer and fewer school-age children. Marty McGuire and I were in the same class—the two of us walking parallel, but not closely, through those grade school years. Marty was an action-seeker, an indifferent student, a guy who would later drive cars fast, swagger sexily down high school halls in his pearl button shirts and tight jeans and try to knock up girls. I was a reader, a serious student, and the sheltered daughter of parents born at the turn of the twentieth century.

After our teacher of four years left and another moved to Iowa after a one-year appointment, Marty and I faced the eighth grade. With Janet going on to high school, the girl next in age to me would be a fourth-grader, the number of students was down to ten, and Marty and I were charging toward adolescence. Mom looked at the situation and began to lobby for Marty, Travis and me, all junior high age, to "go to school in town." The McGuires, the Svensons and the Bishops took us older children out of the school, and it closed, a victim of school consolidation and the declining rural population of Nodaway County.

My mother had not been able to prepare me to face the hostile girls on my first day at Wilcox School, and, even more so, she could not shield me from the withering social judgments of junior high classmates in town. It was sink or swim.

One of the few pieces of information I had about going to Horace Mann was that we would ride to school on a bus. For me, the bus was a magic carpet flying in people and places from the world beyond. Several of my brothers and sisters had attended high school at Horace Mann, boarding the bus each school morning at the local gas station in Wilcox. They emerged silently each afternoon, having swum in the deep waters of their adolescence. The gas station served as a bus stop for buses running between Kansas City and Omaha, as a school bus stop for Horace Mann students, as a place for Dad to "loaf" and play Pinochle in winter, and as a place to pick up A&P coffee or Wonder Bread between weekly shopping trips in Maryville. Brothers Max and Marshall came back from the war on those cream and red Trailways buses. Aunt Emmy, perfectly coiffed, periodically descended from a Kansas City bus carrying an overnight case brimming with perfumes and cosmetics from a city store. Sometimes an order from Sears came from the bowels of the bus, even baby chicks.

During my first years in the Wilcox school, the station was run by Mattie and Johnnie Masters, and while I waited to grip my father around the waist and stand on our Farmall's drawbar to ride home, I sometimes played with the Masters' daughters. When Johnnie died unexpectedly from a heart attack, Mattie gave up the gas station and moved to Maryville with her four daughters. Kim, a year older than I, was graduating from the eighth grade at Horace Mann that spring, so Mom and Mattie arranged for Marty and me to visit junior high with Kim and understand better what lay ahead.

For days before our school visit, I fretted over what outfit to wear. Surely the occasion called for wearing my dressiest outfit from Easter since I was going to go to school in the big city of Maryville. Marty planned to wear his newest and snuggest blue denim jeans and a plaid western shirt studded with pearl snap buttons.

The day before our visit, Mom dropped me off at Mattie's, where I would spend the night before walking to Horace Mann with Kim the next morning. When I excitedly donned my finery the next morning, I saw Kim looking at me with a wrinkled brow. As we walked the three blocks to school, Kim didn't seem to be in that much of a hurry to get there and didn't say much beyond pointing out the campus buildings as we walked across the college commons to Horace Mann. It occurred to me that she wasn't all that thrilled about bringing me to school with her.

Well, we're into it now. We marched up the marble staircase to the junior high room. A woman who would change my life greeted me at the door.

Mrs. Turner, a dowdy triangular-shaped woman, looked like a beige bowling pin in the dowdy skirts and blouses she often wore. Her graying light brown hair was almost the same color as her skin, and I didn't notice right away the keenness of her hazel eyes that missed nothing. Despite her nondescript physical appearance, she was, I would learn that year, brilliant and sometimes dangerously short-tempered, capable of taming the charging hormones of boys like Marty and fiery independent girls like me. Her students feared her, loved her and hated her—no one could come away from her class with a neutral opinion of her and no one who had been in her classes ever forgot her.

As I entered the classroom, I realized that Kim's reluctance to bring her country bumpkin acquaintances to visit the school was well-founded. The students took a long look at Marty's pearl-button shirt and my taffeta skirt and rolled their eyes at each other when Mrs. Turner's back was turned. I could feel the junior high girls' eyes burning into our backs. They looked me up and down with disdain. During recess, I heard one of the girls whisper to Kim, "Where did she get that outfit?

"I don't know," Kim whispered back, mortified. Her mother had obviously twisted her arm to drag me along with her. Throughout the day, I looked at the outfits of the other girls as they casually crossed their legs and laughed carelessly in their knife-pleated plaid skirts, tailored blouses and hose. And they were wearing make-up!

Watching her students take the measure of Marty and me that day, Mrs. Turner was already thinking about what she would have to do to bring Marty and me into the fold of the eighth-graders, most of whom had been together at Horace Mann since kindergarten. The morning crawled past as I, ashamed and miserable, endured the classes. Right after lunch, Marty and I visited the seventh-grade math class with the students who would be our classmates in the fall. Mrs. Turner waded into a review of fractions that no one in the class wanted to think about at all on that warm May afternoon. After a couple of rounds of incorrect answers when students were called upon, and languorous raises of hands, she narrowed her hazel eyes. She began to bark, "What percentage is 1/3?" Students were then supposed to chime the answer in chorus. A smattering responded.

"What percentage is 1/8?" A mixture of uncertain responses, some right, some wrong.

"What is 1/4?" she suddenly turned and asked Marty, who for once in his life was shocked into performing academically. He shot back the correct answer.

"What percentage is 5/8?" she fired at the group.

A few mumbled wrong answers.

Stung by the girls' derision of me and not to be outdone by my classmate of seven years, I heard myself piping up, "62 ½ percent."

Mrs. Turner smirked at the class. "I think you people need some new blood. Our visitors know the answers." Seething and ashamed, our future classmates stared at their desks. Marty and I, rubes though we were, knew that we would have a long road ahead of us the next year.

That fall, Marty and I circled around the edges of the tightly knit classmates who had been together since kindergarten. There were two other new girls in the class who were equally ignored. Mrs. Turner took the occasion to teach the student teachers observing us how to do a sociogram. Everyone in the class had to answer a series of questions, such as listing privately the people they'd most like to sit by in class. Later, in my own teacher education classes, I studied this method, so I now know that Mrs. Turner and the student teachers then drew little affinity circles around those who had listed each other and were left with a list of class waifs on the outside of all circles. Marty, the two new girls and I each orbited alone outside the clusters of circles. To address the issue of our not fitting in, she initiated a "spelling partners" program to break up the cliques and integrate us newcomers into the class, and she created little social studies project groups. In a few weeks, a new, more inclusive eighth-grade class began to emerge.

In Mrs. Turner's spelling program, we had to identify two words in our reading that we didn't know. Then we used these words in a paragraph or short essay that we wrote each night and shared with our spelling partners the next day before turning it in to the cadre of student teachers for grading. Every two weeks, we had a spelling test including our own twenty words. Soon we wrote longer and cleverer pieces as we competed for the moment of glory when our writing was read aloud to the class. This nightly writing assignment was my favorite homework, and though I was not particularly attracted to my mousy spelling partner or her unimaginative prose, I was also a pragmatist. I needed to make a friend.

As a result of Mrs. Turner's social engineering, a small group of us "outsider girls" became friends. One of the girls was Ellie Johnson, child of a single parent and voracious reader; another was Connie York, only daughter of two older parents; the third was Karen Foster, the frumpy, serious daughter of a strait-laced Baptist professor. I suspect Karen was paired with me because she was my peer in spelling ability and equally in need of a friend. It was a precarious alliance of academic achievers, with Karen and Connie being devoutly religious and proper and Ellie and I having an eye for irreverence, mischief and adventure.

The first time that I was invited to spend the night at Karen's house was almost the last. Karen's mother engaged me in conversation. As we talked, I said, "Oh, I think about crap like that," having no idea that "crap" was a word any more loaded than a word like "milk" or "shoes." Her eyes widened in shock.

"We don't use language like that in this home," she said through tight lips.

I knew I'd done something wrong, but I didn't know what. Karen was mortified, on the one hand wanting to please her mother and escape her Baptist righteousness, and, on the other hand, desperately wanting to keep one of the few friends she had. Through the night, I pondered. What had I said? This episode marked my first awareness of differences in language choice from one group to another—everybody at Wilcox School said "crap" whenever they wanted to. The "F-word" was off-limits, but nobody ever mentioned the word "crap" to me. It was just another word for "stuff." I began a careful study of the dress, speech and manners of the "in group" and learned.

About then, Mrs. Turner launched a major annual class project which serendipitously accelerated my study of ways and manners. She believed that an important part of the junior high curriculum was etiquette, so she shaped her English, math and social studies lesson plans around the planning and implementation of a Junior High School Banquet, which the eighth grade held for their faculty, parents and the seventh grade. In the weeks leading up to the banquet, we had to calculate portions of food and budget for the event, laboriously write and re-write invitations (the seventh graders had to write formal acceptances), learn how to set the table properly and fold the napkins (the seventh-graders practiced using them). Every math problem and English assignment focused on the skills required to carry off this event. In music class, we learned new songs to perform the entertainment at the banquet.

It was a huge affair. Marty and I had to do double the amount of work to avoid her public ridicule because we had missed the seventh-grade "manners" curriculum and had to catch up. Our transition into the eighth grade veered between smooth and rough. Each of us was independent and unused to structured classes, and Mrs. Turner capriciously swung between brilliance and cutting outbursts. One year, her etiquette lessons went overboard as she marched humiliated seventh- and eighth-grade boys to the bathroom to wash their sweaty, hormonally enhanced armpits. The story of this shaming passed apoc-ryphally from one apprehensive sixth-grader to the next as they antic-ipated being her captive the following year. After hearing horror sto-ries about Mrs. Turner from their sixth-grade children, some parents quickly arranged for their children to go to Maryville Junior High the next year.

Marty's general strategy for coping with Mrs. Turner was to avoid her notice and do as little as possible. Mine was to compete and achieve, especially in reading and writing.

Everyone in the class belonged to book club, Mrs. Turner's eu-phemistic term for reading class. Each of us had to read two outside reading books of substantial length every six weeks. On Wednesdays, we presented original skits on an episode or chapter in one of our books to classmates. We could also expect to be enlisted as cast mem-bers in others' skits on a regular basis. The skits evolved into elabo-rate competitive events as we incorporated music, costumes and mime into our skits. We listened anxiously to her post-performance critiques, which could exult or damn us for the day. We all wished to be one of her favored smart boys, Stephen Brien or Doug Ballinger, who could do no wrong.

Every six weeks, we stood in a huge semi-circle around the room in descending order of how many pages we had read during the past six weeks. The high achievers competed to be the one standing at the top end; indifferent or poor readers stood at the bottom awaiting her scorn. Ellie set the pace, racking up two thousand pages with books such as *Gone with the Wind*, which Mrs. Turner frowned upon for con-tent but had to acknowledge met the criteria she had set. Ellie got by with reading it, to my relief, since I was halfway through reading the gripping novel. Within weeks, Ellie and I found ourselves shoe-horned into reading the classics. Mrs. Turner may have lost the "Gone with the Wind" battle, but she won the war. One of her gifts was knowing how to "up the ante," but her efforts to pull us along went overboard from time to time.

On the few occasions she aimed a sarcastic jab my way, my chin raised defiantly, my green eyes flashed, and my mouth set in a stubborn line. She once said to me, "Rose Ann, I can always tell when you are mad. Your red hair stands on end."

Critical remarks directed at me, especially if I thought them unjustified, triggered an instant response originating in my refusal to be cowed by my brothers' teasing. When I felt attacked, I vowed to myself, "I will not be broken. I will show him/her/them." Over the years, I've come to hide my anger better, but my inner voice still responds the same way when my dignity is assaulted. This character trait has brought me grief—there are times when I should have taken in the information delivered, no matter how stingingly, and I refused to hear it. Other times my stubborn insistence on refusing to internalize negative messages received from others (rivals, patriarchal authority figures, stifling institutions, and crazy people) helped me find or keep my identity.

Baby Rosie, the youngest and most doted on member of the family, would not be side-lined. In my grade school days, I was the brightest, most creative, and, possibly, most privileged girl in the school, and that was a role I planned to keep even though I had moved to a larger pond.

From the age of five, I had sung solos and given recitations at Wilcox events. When the Christmas program at Horace Mann was in its planning stages, I was stung to find out that I was not given a speaking role or solo of any kind. Surely Miss Miller, the music teacher, had made a mistake, so I took her aside and explained that I wanted to sing "Silver Bells." She looked surprised and unenthusiastic. I don't think she had any plans at all for "Silver Bells" or me to be on the program. By the next day, she agreed that I would be included in the program, probably not wanting to tell me "No."

Miss Miller's Christmas program strongly featured Dolores, a demure, not-too-bright classmate with a stunning coloratura soprano voice. I listened to Dolores's voice in music class, thinking I wanted to learn to sing like that. I had never heard singers make those high, trilling, sparkling sounds, and I made up my mind to learn how to get my voice to have those resonant tones. I sat next to Dolores in music class, matching her tones and notes. By May, I was second only to Dolores in our soprano section. My friend from Wilcox, Travis, found his voice in that class when he was given a solo in selections from *The Marriage of Figaro*, which the junior high chorus was learning to commemorate Mozart's birthday. By the end of the year, Travis and I sat side by side on the school bus each morning, passing the miles with talk about the next choral concert or play.

Bit by bit, we found our ways to swim in these new waters. Marty blended into the bushes at the shoreline while I plunged into the deep water, glorying in the chance to experience everything the school could offer. For Travis, Janet, Marty and me, the events of the larger world went unnoticed. It took all our energy to figure out the complicated social dynamics of the world we had been tossed into. With newly dis-covered hormones, Marty made a couple of half-hearted efforts to get me to play with him in the hay and, getting no encouragement, looked ahead at all the enticing possibilities awaiting his attention at the new school. Janet marched steadfastly forward toward high school, keep-ing a sharp eye out for a husband. Travis and I jumped into the music, drama and field trips to Kansas City, wanting to see more of this slight-ly larger world we'd fallen into.

Scylla and Charybdis

Homer's *The Odyssey* was over-rated, I thought. I couldn't relate to a military guy wandering aimlessly from one disaster to another, apparently unable to learn from his bad experiences or deal with his idiot crewmen. The women, products of male fantasy and, in no way convincing, had no complexities of their own. It was all about Odysseus.

But one part drew my complete attention, the description of Scylla and Charybdis, a monster and a bottomless whirlpool, waiting on either side of a narrow strait. The English teacher said that an old expression, "between the Devil and the deep blue sea," traced its own seventeenth-century roots back to Homer's mythic Scylla and Charybdis. I realized for the first time that my mother's colorful language, replete with such expressions, had a history and existed within an ancient language tradition—that language, like people, was alive with a past, present and future.

The mythic concept of Scylla and Charybdis itself lured me into a world of metaphor that gave words and images to describe what I was feeling as an adolescent trying to decipher where I fit. As I moved toward adulthood, the pressure to define myself as a woman in both sexual and social terms pressed in on me more and more, my Scylla and Charybdis.

Having survived the transition from one-room country school to high school, I was determined to wear stylish clothes, and my mother's excellence as a seamstress made her a willing ally. The clothes were part of the transition. As I struggled to come to terms with my emerging sexuality, I also was coming face to face with the insistent expectations pumped out in film, song, family and community about what it meant to "be a woman." These undefined banks of submerged weeds pulled one way then another beneath the river, pulling at my strong will to learn and achieve.

The summer between eighth grade and my freshman year of high school, I felt the pull of these competing currents. My younger brothers having now left home, my father sorely missed having someone to help him in the fields and proposed that I learn to drive the tractor and pull wagons of grain from the field to the storage bins.

"No," my mother said, clearly digging in her heels. "You've had five sons to help you on the farm. It's my turn. Rosie will stay in the house and help me."

After Dad had gone, chastened, to fill the tractors with gas at the big tank in our drive, she said, "I don't want you working in the fields and ending up with rough, thick hands and tough, sun-burned skin like those Guenther girls."

That summer, my mother began to teach me to do the things I would need to know as an adult—homemaking and childcare. First off, I needed to learn to cook. I remember standing by her side as she began my lesson in bread making.

"Put some flour in a bowl and make a well in the middle of it," she said. "Now add some salt."

"How much?"

"Let me see. No, add some more."

"How do you know how much to add?"

"Well, you just do. Now stir in this hot milk. Not too hot or it will kill the yeast."

"Kill the yeast? Was it alive?" I thought, staring down into the little pan of warmed milk. "How hot?"

She stuck her finger in the middle of the pan of scalded milk. "Not yet. You just know from touching the milk when it's right."

And later, "You just know when you've added enough flour—by the way it feels." I doubtfully pushed the sticky mass back and forth under my hands, hating the way it stuck to my fingers. Mom stuck her hand down into the fifty-pound flour bin at her knee, picked up a fistful of flour and dumped it on the counter beneath the messy dough.

"Knead some more."

Sighing, I kneaded more.

"You can tell when you've kneaded it enough by how it looks. You just know."

Suddenly the dough assumed a rounded shape. She lightly touched her fingers around the side of the ball, giving it a deft quarter turn and kneaded it a few times. There it was, a soft, pliant round ball, smooth as a baby's bottom—an organic living thing waiting to be baked. I'd just had my first formal lesson in cooking by touch and sight, coping with the uncertainty of a work in progress.

A crash course in childcare and homemaking came with the birth of a niece and a nephew. My brother Chad's second baby came in June, and I was sent to his little brick house in Maryville to help their mother when she came home from the hospital.

I slept on an army cot in the living room of the tiny, sweltering post-World War II house, trying not to hear the cries of the baby. The older child, at seventeen months, slept fitfully in the crib taking up the dimensions of his room during the long hot nights. The days began with making baby formula. Kay taught me to invert the baby bottles in a kettle of water on the stove and bring the water to boiling. Steam from the boiling water resulted in a hot, humid kitchen from nine in the morning on. One by one, we fished a sterilized bottle from its boiling bath with a dinner fork and, holding the hot bottle with a dish towel, quickly filled it with the warm formula, popped a sterilized nipple upside down onto the top of the bottle and sealed it tight with a plastic screw-on ring. That business of the day done, the load of diapers we had just washed was ready to hang on lines crossing the back yard. By noon the hot wash and bottle sterilizing heated the tiny house to a humid, stifling 100 degrees.

Over bologna and Rainbow bread sandwiches, Kay and I came up with something I could cook for supper. Though a mother of two, Kay was still a teenager herself and had a limited cooking repertoire. I knew how to cook three things: boiled hot dogs, hamburgers or an oven dinner of baked potatoes and meat loaf. When Manny, the older baby, had finally settled down for his nap, we pored over *True Romance*, or *Hollywood* magazines. Each day seemed the same to me— baby formula, diapers, cooking, washing and ironing in the squat little house on Third Street. I couldn't wait to get back to my books, Broadway musical records and daydreaming in the swing on the farmhouse porch, where there was always a breeze.

I had been home two weeks when the call came from my brother-in-law Stanley in Oklahoma. Laura's third child in three years had just arrived, and my sister needed help. My parents put me on the 11:40 p.m. bus, which would be in Anadarko, Oklahoma, the next day. When the bus first stopped the next morning, we were somewhere in Arkansas. As I sleepily descended the bus steps, my hand rested inadvertently on top of the hand of the middle-aged black man behind me. He jerked his hand away, visibly frightened, and as soon as his foot hit the ground, he hurried away, glancing behind him. As I walked on the sidewalk to the diner, I noticed that all the black people, heads down, got into the street to let me pass. I did not know that one little offended squeal from me would have cost the man his life in this Jim Crow town.

Laura and Stanley had lived in their current apartment for only two months, and it had no homelike touches, but they felt lucky to get the apartment, the first floor of a rundown brick four-square. Town folk mistrusted them as members of the itinerant seismograph crew who had come to the area to look for prospective oil-drilling sites. The walls of the big square rooms were bare, and the landlord provided the least amount of furniture he could get by with. My army cot and suitcase sat in the corner of the living room, which I shared with three-year-old Katy in her crib and a sway-backed maroon velvet couch. Outside the eternally dust-filtered windowpanes, I saw the hard-packed dirt surrounding the house and, here and there, scraggly weeds poking their pitiful heads up through the cracks in the ground.

In the past month of learning the rudiments of what could be my own future work, I had added making macaroni and tomatoes to my cooking repertoire, and during the long hot afternoons between lunch and dinner, I baked a white cake for dessert, adding several degrees to the stifling temperature in the apartment. When there were big splats of raindrops falling through the hot air to the sheets stiffly hanging from the lines in the back yard, I raced outside to retrieve the sheets before dust spots stuck to the swiftly evaporating raindrops. In the simmering heat, the sugary aroma of the white cake blended with the faint smell of urine and Clorox in the diaper pail.

If there was money and Stanley wasn't too exhausted from his long day in the field, we all piled into the car, windows down, toddlers Katy and Ava perched beside me on the seats my sister had made by tying together four tall juice cans and upholstering them in broadcloth. My sister bottle-fed Eric in the front seat, nodding distractedly as Stanley talked about his day. Those little jaunts to the Dairy Queen with the evening air pouring through the car windows were the best part of the visit. The tedium of the days disabused me of the romantic notions I had of my sister, pretty, young and in love, roaming freely from place to place. Was this what all the romance magazines added up to?

The summer's events simmered in my brain as I pondered the meaning of the pronounced new curves in my body and my reluctant apprenticeships in childcare and housekeeping. Only a few weeks after Stephen Brien's gentle sexual advance, I'd encountered my neighbor Charlie, newly returned from the Army, and ran from his lust. My brother, who had just returned from Korea, studied me as I passed by his rocking chair on my way to the mailbox. "Her lipstick is all wrong," he said. "That loud pink clashes with her red hair." Unspoken was, "if she's ever going to attract guys like me." I was expected to learn to cook and make baby formula—and look good to men. I was plunged headlong into a sexual world that confused, attracted and frightened me all at once.

A girlfriend in town invited me to see *Love Me Tender*—"WITH ELVIS PRESLEY!" she shrieked over our party line telephone. All I knew about Elvis Presley I had heard from my music teacher who said that he was vulgar and lacking in musical technique. My nerdy girl self wanted to put my hands over my ears and refuse to listen to such an untalented oaf; my teenager self wanted to fit in with my friends and scream in adoration of his animal vitality.

During the summer, I was drawn again into the rhythms of the farm. When Dad brought in haying or threshing crews on hot summer days, Mom and I were the kitchen crew. Mom began preparing the dinner for eight to twelve people immediately after breakfast. I buried my head in my pillow, waiting for her to call up the stairway, "Are you going to stay in bed all day? Get down here and help."

I dragged my sluggish teenaged body downstairs and ate my toast while I watched my mother already in full production at the kitchen counter. After thirty years' practice, she mixed and kneaded the two loaves of bread and four pans of rolls with hardly a wasted motion.

As soon as she had covered the plump lumps of dough with a dish towel and left them to rise, she moved on to the pies. Within an hour, she popped two to four pies—cream pies topped with snowy meringue and cherry or peach pies—into the oven and wiped off counters, punched down the bread dough to rise a second time and directed me to wash the breakfast and baking dishes.

While I washed the dishes, she got out a large mixing bowl and dumped several cups of flour into it. She scooped out a well in the flour and broke eggs into it, working from a formula in her head. As she worked the mixture with her hands, the dough began to form into a cohesive mass. Quickly turning the dough onto the floured countertop, she reached into the fifty-pound capacity flour bin in the cabinet for the fat rolling pin, its handles long ago broken off, and began to roll the noodle dough into a large oval. She rolled the oval into a cylinder and cut the noodle dough into fat fingers, spreading them across the counter to dry. Her granddaughter called them "Grandma's good old tough noodles."

She again "cleaned up her mess" at the kitchen counter, tossing more bowls and knives into the dishwater for me to wash. The pies came out of the oven; the bread went into the oven. She dispatched me to the garden to pull up the radishes and green onions and, in their season, dig up the turnips and pick the tomatoes, green beans or peas. We washed, trimmed, sliced, and hulled the vegetables and put them to rest in a bowl until dinner.

The next step was putting the roast on to cook. She seared the outsides of the chuck roast on each side, then added water to the pot, bringing the water to a boil before turning the heat down, plunked the lid on and watched me over the half-wall dividing the kitchen from the dining room. I was assigned to extend the dining room table to its full length, lugging in heavy table leaves from the laundry room. To cover the long table, I spread two tablecloths end to end.

With the roast well on its way to becoming fork-tender shreds of beef chunked on the plate, she began to watch for the mail carrier to edge his old green Chevy up to the mailbox at the side of the gravel road. Once he'd left the day's mail for me to bring to the house, she sorted through it. Together we read any letters that had arrived from Max or Laura, and she thumbed through a *Kitchen Klatter*, *Capper's Weekly*, *Saturday Evening Post* or *Farm Journal*, periodically glancing up at the clock.

By eleven o'clock, we moved back into action. By quarter after eleven, Mom had the huge kettle of potatoes peeled and set to boil. "If you want dinner at noon, you start your potatoes at quarter after eleven," she said to me, anticipating a day when I would be the shop foreman of my own kitchen. I set the table, filled the glasses with tea or lemonade, placed sliced cheddar planks, butter and jelly at each end of the long expanse, sliced the bread, and delivered the bowls of sliced tomatoes and raw vegetables to the table. Finally, I cut each pie into six wedges.

During this time, Mom cooked the noodles in the steaming broth of the roast, mashed the potatoes, carefully saving some potato water to add to the gravy, made the gravy and cooked her vegetable side dishes. At five to twelve, the men began to file into the back porch, in turn washing their sunburned faces topped by a broad white strip of skin on their foreheads where their caps had been. Mom was a stickler for prompt arrival—"Breakfast is at six, dinner is at twelve, and supper is at 5:30. I go to the trouble to cook it on time, and I expect you to be here to eat it on time—while it is hot and good."

While the other men washed their dust-matted sweaty arms, Dad leaned against the counter watching Mom dish up the hot food. She summarized the contents of the day's mail and any phone calls that had come in during the morning. My job was to haul extra chairs in from the laundry room or closet and place them around the table. The men positioned themselves at the table, with Dad at the head. Mom and I reserved the corner nearest the kitchen for ourselves, "the jumping up place," so we could stoke the human furnaces seated at the table. Within minutes, it was time to take their orders for dessert: which pie, with or without ice cream, with or without a slice of cheddar or a splotch of cream poured over the top of a fruit pie crust.

The crew sprawled on the shaded east side of the lawn, toothpicks hanging from their mouths, desultorily commenting on the weather, the condition of the crop, some neighborhood gossip. For a few minutes, Dad catnapped in the grass, his hips two triangles of white flesh flashing from the point where his chambray shirt and old blue overalls did not meet. While my father and brothers filled the tractors with gas and made minor repairs or adjustments to the equipment, Mom and I washed and dried the dishes, shook out the tablecloths and whisked them into the laundry, removed the table leaves, put away any remaining food and returned the chairs to their spots.

By one-fifteen, Mom had curled up on a living room couch to nap. Participating in her fierce efficiency with large-scale farm dinner production was a course in project management that I applied throughout my career. On that afternoon, my only thought concerned getting a chance to dip back into my library book. I lay on the other couch, my feet swung up over its back, and pulled toward me the book resting open with its spine up on the couch back. I was free at last to find out whether Ashley Wilkes ever got any gumption or if Scarlett would ever understand that dark, seductive Rhett loved her more than Ashley ever would.

Wellsprings

In the stack of postcards and snapshots my brother gave me, I see my friend Veronica smiling sleepily at me. I had thrown a magnificent slumber party at the end of the summer. Seven classmates and I, on the eve of beginning high school and its rites of passage, sprawled on mattresses laid on our rambling front porch, having stuffed ourselves with hot dogs roasted over a huge bonfire. We danced like banshees around the fire, screaming so loudly that the gas station owner in Wilcox, a mile away, heard us. Throughout the dark night, with locusts humming in the background, we yelled, giggled, threw pillows, drank Coke, and finally whispered our private thoughts to each other until five in the morning.

The rip-roaring success of this party solidified the friendship of us eight girls into a voting bloc that elected me freshman class president that September. Despite the swirl of confusion surrounding my female identity, I found my footing. My parents' native intelligence, work habits and initiative—their steady voices—let me move with the current moving me into ever deeper, broader waters.

My spirits have lifted as the Missouri valley falls farther and farther behind me. I sit on a picnic table bench near Winterset, Iowa, about halfway home. I see my father, competitive and resourceful—a superb checkers player—leaning over the red and black pieces and relishing the moment he would swoop down and sweep five checkers from his opponent's field in a single move. At the age of ninety-five, he jumped at the chance to lure a visitor into playing him.

Pointing at the board, he asked, "Is that one black or red?"

Macular degeneration had eaten away his vision, but not his mind for strategy. On hearing that it was his color, "red," his thick work-swollen hands moved with quick grace to jump three checkers, chuckling over the success of the trap he'd laid.

I hear his voice coaching me in Pinochle. He never "let me" win—I had to earn every victory.

"The ace has already been played. You play the 10 of trumps. That will force the other guy to have to spend a bigger face card. If your partner has a bigger trump, you'll get the play. If there are still face cards out there, the third player will have to use it to take the round. Either way helps you. If the cards are distributed evenly, by the time your turn comes again, you'll be able to trump any play at will with the Jack that is in your hand."

He loved a challenge, and because of his strategic sense, he won far more often than he lost. When he'd get up on a February morning to see our road drifted closed, he was compelled to go somewhere— anywhere. The whole point was having a reason to battle the drifts on his "M" Farmall, his "C" being too small for the task of bucking and breaking through the drifts. On school-day mornings after a snowstorm, he charged the drifts on his tractor, reaching the crest of McGuire's hill at last, then he'd come back to the house for me to climb on the seat in front of him while Marty stood on the toolbox behind and held on to the tractor seat for the ride to school. Dad had conquered his Everest for the morning.

Mom met challenges with equal alacrity, but where Dad was strategic, she was spirited, witty and resourceful. I see her standing on the sloping roof of our house and vigorously polishing the bedroom windows on the second story. As she polished, the exhausted prewar elastic in her underpants gave way. Chad and I rolled on the ground kicking our feet and laughing, unable to stop. Mom stepped deftly out of one of the panty legs drooping around her ankles, caught the other leg on the toe of her foot and tossed them to her right hand. Then, waving them grandly at us, she turned back to the window, continued to apply Bon Ami to it in large white circles and polish the cleaner off with the panties.

On a windy June morning, the cherries needed picking. Mom told me to climb to the top and get them. The top branches waved back and forth in the wind, and soon I was dizzy and nauseous with motion sickness. She took my place, and at the age of sixty, climbed to the top of the tree, positioned one foot on each of two big branches and, bobbing and swaying with the tree, brought buckets of cherries down.

She was not a patient woman. After waiting too long, in her mind, for a job to get done, she fumed, "If you want something done right or on time, you're going to have to do it yourself." That statement preceded wallpapering, painting rooms, having her children stand on the end of a board to counterbalance her as she stood on the other end above an open staircase to paint the ceiling above it.

Despite adolescent angst and social awkwardness, I entered high school, with my parents' verve for meeting challenges head-on, self-directed focus, and a desire to see what was over the next hill. For nine months of the year throughout high school, Wilcox and the farm barely existed. I ate and slept there, otherwise diving into new experiences the school opened for me.

I began my freshman year of high school with hormones pounding, heart trembling and a brain on fire with the new ideas delivered, as if on a silver platter, every single day by my teachers. Whether dissecting frogs, visualizing Miss Havisham in her ghastly room, singing in a chorus of forty voices, or writing, I was transported into worlds I had not known existed.

The required Home Economics class was a glaring exception to my happiness with my classes. The independence and self-reliance I had learned both in my country school and at home were detriments here. Mrs. Samson, a prim, plodding technician, infuriated me. How insulting to have to "learn" how to boil an egg! We spent six weeks making a simple gathered skirt that my mother whipped out in thirty minutes. Mrs. Samson imposed the standards of a professional seamstress on us regardless of what we were making. The pinking of seams in a cotton dirndl skirt was an excessively persnickety waste of time. Night after night, students were sent home to rip out ragged, crooked seams and do them again. I seethed. Mrs. Samson took me aside and commented that the two of us didn't seem to get along, that I had to be dragged truculently along at every step. She was right. I hated every minute of the tedious class and saw no reason that I should have to endure it. I went to the school principal and asked for the requirement to be waived.

Mr. Dieterich knew through prior experience with my brothers and sisters that we were an independent lot and needed to be channeled into positive behaviors carefully.

"All right. Why don't you take Beginning Journalism instead?"

It was an inspired suggestion. Spared further futile, tense interactions with Mrs. Samson and her pinking shears, I dove into headlines, bylines, ads, picas and the "editorial we."

Learning and achieving routed me through my confused struggle to discover who I could become. I caught glimpses of another life for me through school events.

My Spanish teacher, a stern, bad-tempered man, invited the Honor Society to his house. He toured us through his house, pointing out his two grand pianos.

"This one belongs to Mrs. Dredge. We have divided the house in two so that we get along well."

My friends and I looked furtively at each other. His elegant furnishings, artwork and divided household carried us into a world we had never encountered. Mrs. Dredge glared at all of us, not speaking, from her side of the house.

"So," I thought, "In this world, you don't even have to *pretend* to like each other."

Our teachers, most of whom taught at the college level, understood that we came from homes where none of this was possible, whether it was original art or an unconventional approach to marriage. Crotchety old Dr. Dredge despised the high school class he was forced to endure as part of his teaching load at the college. He took pleasure in emphasizing his cultural superiority and "shocking our little minds." In my high school class of twenty, there were no children of professionals. All of us came from farms and blue-collar workers in town. The professors' children I had met on my first visit at Horace Mann had moved to bigger places. The two wealthiest people in our class were the children of the two rival car dealers in town. If there were any parents who decided to divide their house into two parts, they certainly didn't talk about it. My parents were most impressed with my report on his married life and gleefully told their friends across the Pinochle table that Saturday night about what those college professors in town were doing.

For my part, I did not forget the glistening grand pianos and tastefully framed art on the walls, and apparently, my brother Max hadn't forgotten them either. Dr. Dredge had been his Spanish teacher when Max attended the college on the GI Bill. Years later, when he heard Dr. Dredge had died, he bought his grand piano and had it shipped to California. When I visited my brother there, I saw delicate blue and white porcelain figurines reminiscent of those in the Dredges' separate living rooms. Dr. Dredge's quietly elegant house somehow signified a life both my brother and I wanted to live.

Teachers took a busload of students to Kansas City to see "Ben Hur" in Cinemascope. My friend Ellie and I spent days planning what we would wear. We no longer wore can-cans and poodle skirts but felt sophisticated and fashionable in dark wool sheath dresses, pointed-toe high heels with hose, and rhinestone pins and earrings.

We hobbled around The Country Club Plaza, smiling bravely as the backs of our heels chafed and our toes screamed for freedom. Our girdles mercilessly squeezed our slender hips and thighs, their formidable satin panels cutting mercilessly into our stomachs, but I absorbed the sights, sounds and tastes all around me. At Wolferman's Cafeteria, there were enormous tables of exotic food stretching the length of the restaurant. The Plaza, the nation's first planned shopping center, burst with neo-Roman statues spouting water from their mouths and mammoth fountains marking intersections. Red velvet curtains draped elegantly around subdued sconces on the walls of the giant theater. I wanted more.

The new minister at the church in Wilcox provided a way for me to go further afield, both geographically and metaphorically. Reverend Tim Hutton, young and handsome, came to the Wilcox Methodist Church for his first pastoral assignment. He and his wife took on the task of recruiting "the young people," and Rev. Tim Hutton immediately recognized me as one of the more influential teenagers in the community. He tapped into my high school leadership experience and my love of singing. Soon I worked with him on the monthly church newsletter and became choir director for the "Youth Choir," a vastly exaggerated designation. In fact, every young person attending Sunday school from the age of five to eighteen was in the motley choir, taking the place of the adult church choir once a month. Rev. Tim sent me off to a regional church conference to learn how to direct a youth choir, and I came back with the basic concept that church music existed to advance theology and needed to fit the singers' ages.

As I listened to the lectures, I realized that adolescent boys slouched in their chairs and, undoubtedly thinking of sex, would not be theologically advanced by singing the kindergarten chestnut "Jesus Loves Me." The concept seemed innocent enough, but my introduction of new songs into the Sunday school routine and my outrageous notion that we might practice these songs more than one time in advance released a firestorm. Incensed church elders met with the minister and demanded that I stop upsetting the order of things. When Tim spoke to me about the issue, I immediately resigned as choir director and stopped attending church.

I was happy to be finished with religion as I had experienced it. "Faith" and "Belief" had nothing to do with my church attendance as a child or teenager. Sunday school and the annual week of Bible school had been avenues for socializing. Each June, some of the younger women in the Wilcox Church organized the neighborhood children into classes by age and we, regardless of whether our parents ever attended church, gathered to color, hear stories, dramatize Bible stories and, best of all, play games outside. By third grade, I thought the stories flowing from the mouths of the teachers were a little unbelievable. How could somebody live through being swallowed by a whale? How could a full-grown woman be made out of only one man's rib? What was this about a single loaf of bread feeding *multitudes*? One day after Bible school, I approached my father as he read the daily newspaper in his reclining rocker.

"Is that story about Jonah and the whale true?"

"Well, I always had a little trouble believing that, too."

It was a secret he and I shared. The next day at Bible school, I participated in the games and songs, knowing that I could let the teachers tell their stories, but I didn't have to believe them.

One sultry summer week, a revival minister from Oklahoma came to Wilcox, and Janet and Travis, children of pious parents, asked me to attend. I was curious, and the opportunity to go out at night was irresistible. The three of us arrived at the church a little later than the others, so we found benches near the back of the church. Up front, the minister was pacing back and forth behind the altar, waving his hands, and dramatically talking about how he was saved. Being saved seemed to be pretty important to not frying in Hell. I could not stop looking at his oily slicked back hair and sweat-drenched face. His thin polyester shirt clung to his back and chest. When he lifted his arms, drops flowed down his arms and dripped off his elbows. Adults I had known all my life were becoming agitated, occasionally nodding vigorously and shouting "Amen!" Their actions were unlike anything I'd ever seen from my parents' stoical friends. People began to walk down the church aisle toward the minister as he stood before a pan of water, dipping his hands in it to dump over the heads of the farmers and their wives. Their fervor created a mounting pressure for others to show their faith and go down the aisle, but I could never do that. I quietly slid off the bench and out the side door and waited in the dark to be taken home. After that week, church members went back to their usual work and their usual church services as if nothing had happened, and I think nothing had.

As I reflected on the ease with which I walked away from the church, I knew that it wasn't the church I loved—it was Rev. Tim Hutton himself. As a preacher supporting "new ideas" at the church, he was under fire, too, and so it was actually easier for him as well as for me if I became a "fallen away Christian." Within a year, he was gone to another assignment. Neither of us ever looked back.

Having escaped Sunday school in Wilcox and my home economics class in town, my days at school were a cornucopia of worlds to discover and new pinnacles to reach. My literature textbooks filled my imagination with glorious sentences, intriguing characters and gripping stories. And I was assigned to write! As editor of the high school newspaper, I basked in the unimaginable luxury of being asked to clothe the world in words. I could see myself becoming a savvy journalist traveling the world to scoop up important news stories or a musical comedy star on Broadway. Travis and I began private voice lessons, leading to our learning to harness sound to resonate effortlessly through the auditoriums, local television shows and area churches where we performed.

The choral director at the university invited Travis and me to join the college cast as members of the chorus and stage dancers in a production of "Brigadoon." We stood in the wings offstage, breathlessly soaking in every note produced by the lead singers and imagining ourselves in their places. We could do this.

With our musical aspirations, Travis and I were already behind the curve. The dominance of stirring orchestral music in Biblical epics was fading, and attendance at Broadway musicals was falling. Movie moguls had been producing star-studded thundering Biblical epics such as *The Robe* in the hope of stemming the tide of television as the medium flooded into every home. Long-haired moody singers with single guitars in dark smoky coffee houses eclipsed folksy *Oklahoma*. Rock and Roll, with its sexy, charged rhythms, expressed a new sensibility. *The Man in the Gray Flannel Suit* and *The Coney Island of the Mind* exuded the angst and alienation underlying the wholesome "all is well" society exemplified by Pat Boone and Debbie Reynolds in *Tammy*.

Absorbed in my music and writing, I noticed nothing of the Civil Rights Movement. I had never heard of the Domino Theory or that the precursors of the Seals were already in Viet Nam. I didn't hear warnings about the "military-industrial complex" or give much thought to the Cold War. Without realizing it, I was riding on a boat plunging obliviously through the 1950s toward massive social change brought about by the end of segregation, a war, the triumph of mass culture and the death of the small farm. Not knowing any smart, strait-jacketed suburban housewives, I had not yet stared directly into the face of what the choices for women were in my place and time.

The Launch

My decision to go to college caused massive battles behind my parents' bedroom door. I only knew about them because of the banging of kitchen cupboard doors and my mother's nearly inaudible annoyed sniffing and sighing as she turned the eggs and poured the juice. My father looked down at his plate and said nothing. My father had to quit school after the fifth grade and, because he was a successful farmer, did not believe his children needed a college education. My mother had, for her time and place, an advanced education, two years of high school. Her father had insisted that she could continue to board in town and attend high school only if she agreed to become a teacher. My mother refused to agree, perhaps having already noticed the handsome red-haired boy a couple of farms away and concluded her formal education then and there.

Years earlier, when my father objected to my oldest brother's going to college, Mom went to war.

"That boy is brilliant. Not meant to be someone's farmhand. He's going to college."

Marshall did begin college only to have it cut short by World War II and the draft. When he returned from the war, the GI Bill provided the money he needed to avoid a lifetime on a farm somewhere nearby. My mother was right about Marshall's brains. He rose to a position as Vice-President for Investment at a bank in Omaha. My father was right about his oldest son's heart. When Marshall retired, he bought eighty acres of land and spent his days happily mowing the expansive green lawn and inhaling its new-mown fragrance on his gentleman's farm. My mother used to say of him, "You can take the boy out of the farm, but you can't take the farm out of the boy."

Was the same true of farm girls?

Now, twenty years later, it was my turn, and Mom went into battle once again. I had won a Regents' scholarship to the local teachers' college. I could live at home, she told Dad, and use that scholarship to learn to make a living for myself. I was a bright girl, and there was no prospective husband in sight. My father finally agreed, probably knowing from long experience that when my mother had set her mind to something, it would be better to just give in. Before this round of arguments, there had been battles over my getting a $2.00 a week allowance in addition to the $1.25 required for school lunches. Then she went to war over my right to wear slacks to school on cold days the way my classmates did. She stared my father down when he started to voice objections to my wearing lipstick, hose and heels. Her baby was going to fit in and, moreover, go to college. Mom prevailed, but I had to agree to stay home and commute to classes to keep the college bills down.

When I began college, freshman hazing was at its zenith. During a week of college initiation, we freshmen were hauled by the hundreds into the gym for tests, lectured at by various deans, and placed in line around the perimeters of the gym to get our registration cards signed. Cheerleaders handed out green and white freshman beanies. A swaggering athlete in a letter jacket told us we had to wear the beanies and appear at the bell tower every Tuesday and Thursday until Homecoming in October. Or else.

"If you don't and we catch you, you'll pay big time," he smirked, feeling his power.

For about three weeks, I went along with this routine. The "Bearcats" (football players) picked pretty, giggling girls from the crowd and forced them to lead cheers, which the hundreds of freshmen dutifully chanted "to build school spirit," the athletes claimed. Meanwhile, they were eying the breasts and ankles of the new crop of Saturday night dates. I stood in the circles of students at the back, not wanting their notice—not that they would have noticed. I wore dark-rimmed glasses and walked around as a commuting student carrying armloads of books—definitely not what they were looking for.

Some men were also sought out for special attention—some because they looked imminently tormentable and others because they positioned themselves in the front rows hoping to be known by rush week and courted into fraternities. They had to lead cheers, crawl around on their hands and knees doing obeisance to the athletes or get hosed down with cold water when they did not perform to standard. Of course, there was no way to meet the unknown standard, so they all got hosed down. Some students who had not appeared at the bell tower at the appointed hour were dragged from dorm rooms and cafeterias for public humiliation and week-long punishments.

Watching coolly from the back, I figured out that this ritual was not designed to include someone like me. If I were careful, I would never be missed. I decided that the next Thursday I would remove my beanie right after my class got out at 11:30. Because the athletes sometimes cruised past the all-freshman classes, I didn't dare take off the beanie during my morning classes. I went where these upperclassmen would never think to look: the library. I hid in a carrel in the stacks every lunch hour until Homecoming and, as I had suspected, was never missed at the hazing court at the foot of the bell tower.

My freshman year propelled me down the path of ultimately rejecting Maryville. After bathing in the support and encouragement of my high school teachers, my sudden removal from the small pond of twenty students and a circle of close friends at graduation into a bigger pool disconcerted me. My social network was gone as well: Ginny was in Kansas City, Connie had gone to nursing school, Travis had transferred to Kansas University and Jake was in the Navy. New friendships did not develop as the people I knew transferred, dropped out, got married and moved on.

I might have adjusted to early adulthood and had a more satisfying social life had I stayed in a dorm in college, but that was not part of the deal I had struck with my parents. Also, my spirit rebelled against the thought of having to observe the dorm rules. I had never had "hours," and I did not want to start. College women were required to stay in dormitories or, after the freshman year, approved off-campus housing. On Mondays at Northwest, freshman women were required to be in their rooms by 8:00 p.m. Sundays, Tuesdays and Thursdays had a 10:00 p.m. curfew. On Friday and Saturday nights, Cinderella's coach turned into a pumpkin at midnight It galled me that college men, on the other hand, roamed the town like lovesick tomcats, drinking, milling around and instigating panty raids on the girls' dorms. Helen Gurley Brown's *Sex and the Single Girl* did not hit the press for another two years, but I would have been simultaneously attracted to and shocked by her outrageous maxim, "Good girls go to heaven. Bad girls go everywhere."

Getting a role in the first college play of the season offset my sense of anonymity and isolation. For once, my red hair and freckles worked to my advantage in getting a plum role. The director of the production was looking for a young-looking girl to play the fourteen-year-old tomboy in *Time Out for Ginger*. I was the ginger-haired girl he needed, and he may have remembered me from my ardent performance as a chorus member in *Brigadoon* the previous spring.

Theater, music and studying became my life. For three years (I cut my undergrad years at Northwest as short as I could), I got up to study at 4:30, drove into town to classes, got back to the farm in time for supper and returned for play practice from seven to ten. Too shy and sheltered to find a way to fit in with or get to know the dorm dwellers, I threw myself into my studies, music and theater. As much as my father had objected to my going to college, he savored the newspaper stories about my college performances and sat in the fifth row of the theatre on opening night, beaming and rubbing his huge hands together with pleasure.

Millie, a friend from high school, and I wrote and performed in lecture recitals throughout our college years. Our first recital combined Millie's piano and my singing of medieval troubadour songs. Both of us read from *The Canterbury Tales*, interspersing the readings with mini-talks about the philosophy and culture of the time. Our second year's program on Impressionist literature, music, and philosophy solidified our reputations as two of the campus' precious few intellectuals. Millie played Debussy and read Baudelaire poems and I sang period art songs and read the poetry of Rimbaud and Verlaine. Typically, only music majors gave full-length senior recitals, but because of our performance innovations, we were given permission to present a program of modern poetry, piano, and art songs. My mother got into the act, sewing compatible gold recital gowns for each of us.

As we wrote and performed our concerts, we were trying to move beyond the college's offerings by teaching ourselves.

I sought out the competent teachers and tried to avoid the worst. Most of my college teachers were mediocre, having been dragged in from God knows where to teach the GIs flooding into the college after World War II. By the early Sixties, they were firmly established, tenured professors drifting amiably around the regional college, accountable to no one for anything. Women professors hardly existed except in corners reserved for spinsters and trapped wives of low aspiration—Women's Physical Education, Home Economics, Freshman Composition, and French.

Northwest was a dark, little-known corner of academia where professors fired elsewhere for incompetence or malfeasance could hide and be paid for it. Any teachers of promise who strayed into this misbegotten place put in a year or two and left as quickly as they could. One of the legendary full professors who finished out his career at Northwest was Dr. Foxworth, formerly an actor at the Pasadena Rose Theater, as he reminded us daily. He did not care about anything but the stage and the bomb shelter he was building in his basement. At one of his cast parties, he gave us a tour of the bomb shelter he had built beneath his basement floor. Dr. Foxworth's bomb shelter was an expensive model stocked with food and a toilet. As I looked into the claustrophobic concrete cell, I wondered why he would want to be alive after the nuclear holocaust or suffer through the aftermath promised in current magazine articles.

In describing the bomb shelter hysteria of the late 1950s and early 1960s, David Greenburg wrote, "Off and on until the early '60s, Americans built underground rooms that promised to protect them from a nuclear attack. Playing on traditional imagery of women as domestic caretakers, the FCDA pitched housewives advertisements for 'Grandma's Pantry,' a home shelter that women should stock with canned goods, first-aid kits and flashlights. Commercial firms marketed a range of safehouses that ranged from a '$13.50 foxhole shelter' to a $5,000 'deluxe' model that included a phone, beds, toilets and even a Geiger counter." *Life* magazine ran a story on a young newlywed couple who spent their honeymoon in a steel and concrete room twelve feet underground. 'Fallout can be fun,' the article said. Even a bomb shelter needed its own little homemaker.

I viewed the shelter skeptically. I was more inclined to the sanity of the approach described by a neighbor just returned from Army basic training. Some soldier had placed a banner above the door of the mess hall:

IN CASE OF NUCLEAR ATTACK

1. Spread your legs.
2. Put your head between your knees.
3. Bend over.
4. Kiss your ass goodbye.

Most students at our remote state college headed home every weekend. Sorority and fraternity members more often stayed in Maryville to find ways around the rules and party in the frat houses. For me, weekends meant catching up with schoolwork, much of it drilling and memorizing trivial details for Dr. Foxworth.

To pass his classes, students were required to memorize his textbooks, which we took turns reading aloud in class. He took passages from the text and deleted key words from the sentences his secretary typed. During the exam, we had to fill in the blanks and were awarded grades according to the percentage of blanks we filled in correctly. One of his more challenging courses was Anatomy and Physiology of the Hearing and Speaking Mechanisms, for which we had to memorize large sections of *Gray's Anatomy* for his mid-term and final, the only grades in the course other than one for attendance. Daphne, a classmate who belonged to a sorority, was able to crib a copy of these exams from the sorority files but still wasn't motivated enough to memorize the answers. The remainder of us whispered passages of *Anatomy* backstage as we feverishly struggled to memorize major passages. Dr. Foxworth taught all theater classes, so there was no escape.

All afternoon we built stage sets, and every evening we practiced for the upcoming production. Foxworth's demands were excessive and, finally, even the Dean realized he had to rein him in. He became too intense during rehearsal and slapped the leading lady. Another time, the entire cast marched to the president's office after being held in rehearsal until after two o'clock for several nights.

Foxworth's "teaching method" resembled the practice of the notorious ed psych professor who somehow persuaded his wife to come home from her clerical job at the Driver's License Bureau and type his lecture notes verbatim from a textbook. If we were awake enough in the ed psych class, we heard his droning voice read, without a questioning pause, of future dates and events that had occurred years earlier. Obviously, he wasn't awake either.

Another infamous professor at the college was the chair of the English Department, Dr. Robbins, who somehow bumbled into the college from New York City. Whenever women students heard his nasal Brooklyn voice in the hall, they ducked into the nearest classroom. Dr. Robbins's main business in the classroom halls was to cop a feel. He stood by the water fountain, engaging trapped women students and their boyfriends in conversation. He put his arm around the young woman needing to pass his History of the English Language class and worked his fingers ever closer to clasping her breast as her mortified boyfriend looked on helplessly.

Out of this mess of professors in my major and minor fields, Dr. Flood was my favorite. Completely unsuited for teaching at Northwest, his snowy white hair, his stammer, and his height of five feet underscored his mismatch at the college. He had moved to the college from UCLA with his mother, who in her youth had been a prominent ballet dancer. The two of them lived as recluses in a closely shuttered house near the college.

His own feet turned out from early years of ballet training and the resulting waddle, along with other disjointed effeminate mannerisms, made students preparing to teach English at Ravenwood and Skidmore flee into the classes of others. Sometimes Millie and I were the only students enrolled in his upper-level English classes. We liked him because he referred to literary theory and research outside the constraints of historical criticism espoused by our other professors. We leaned forward in his classes trying to understand his stumbling, muttered introductory remarks, then listened as he read Wordsworth and Keats, tears tumbling down his face. Our way of learning from him was to learn from each other. We read his extensive reading assignments and discussed them between ourselves, taking as our discussion cue any key terms we thought we heard him say at the beginning of his lectures.

When I drove into Maryville at dawn for classes, elm fence posts sticking up out of the snowdrifts marked the roadway. Bare-branched trees in distant fence rows fringed like eyelashes delineated the winter fields standing against the blue-gray horizon. Tired and preoccupied with planning the day ahead, I barely saw them. The warm car was a sealed envelope carrying me from the farm to the college seven miles away. I was a boarder in my childhood home now, at home only a few hours of the week to sleep and eat. My parents, their nest almost empty after more than forty years of marriage, basked in their freedom to make road trips to visit grown children or enjoy a slower pace.

I carved intense sixteen-to-eighteen-hour days out of my sleeping hours to study for exams and hastily prepare classes. Getting up at 4:30 a.m. to a cold silent house, I crept down the stairs and replenished the wood in the cast-iron stove squatting in the dining room.

Propping my feet on the andirons, I studied, occasionally peeking around the corner to see my sleeping parents spooned together in their bed. They were still in love, a future I hoped for myself but could not see anywhere in sight.

That last year of college, Millie played the young woman abandoned by her feckless suitor in *Washington Square*, while I flitted across the stage as the departed wife in *Blithe Spirit*. Greg, a freshman music major with a soaring tenor voice, and I began dating during the rehearsals of *Girl Crazy* when we played the romantic leads. At Northwest, we lived in a bell jar removed from the trends rocking the art world. We didn't know who Bob Dylan was or that his debut album that year would make Broadway musicals seems as quaint as buggies. The most startling pop culture revolution in our musical lives was the incursion of the rhythm-and-blues-based Twist onto the dance floor where we danced to "La Vie en Rose" at the Valentine Ball.

The music we were more aware of playing in all our backgrounds was "life after" the show, our futures. Millie was engaged to be married, so she and her fiancée made plans to pursue their graduate degrees at the University of Missouri. Greg wanted to move to Omaha in the summer to play in Summer Stock. The prospect of teaching English in a tiny high school around Maryville and marrying a local farmer spurred me to apply to graduate school at the University of Missouri and the University of Kansas, those schools being as far as my imagination reached at that point.

I turned to Dr. Flood for advice as I neared graduation. Although he was my advisor from whom I had to get a signature for my schedule each semester, I'd long before given up on trying to find him in the press of registration and had forged his signature for several semesters. Still, I thought, he might be able to give me some advice.

"What can I do if I don't teach high school English? What is a master's degree for? Maybe I could do that?"

He looked at me in complete shock, and I felt instantly embarrassed and silenced by his stare.

"Why I don't know," he answered, studying my face in disbelief.

Had he always simply thought I'd teach high school in Maryville? Had he never considered the question before? Was he mortified for me because I didn't know what a master's degree was?

We both turned and walked away, him to his office to read Wordsworth and me to my car to drive back to the farm.

I had no idea what people did with a master's degree but getting a scholarship would be a way to go to the University of Kansas and escape Nodaway County at last. I didn't know I had a soul mate out there, a child of the Ozarks, Helen Gurley Brown: "I never liked the looks of the life that was programmed for me—ordinary, hillbilly and poor—and I repudiated it from the time I was seven years old," she wrote in her book *Having It All* (1982).

The decision to go to graduate school occasioned renewed talk behind the bedroom door between my parents. My father was sure that I would never amount to anything and would never stop going to school, which he was not willing to bankroll any longer. It was now time for me to get serious about life.

When I was offered a scholarship to Kansas, I snatched it, secure in knowing that Travis was going there, and I would have someone to help me transition to the major university 140 miles from Maryville. After hearing about my plan to go to Lawrence, Dad glowered at me over breakfast.

"Having four boyfriends is having no boyfriends at all," he said, alluding to the four men I'd dated either in close succession or simultaneously during my last semester at the college. He was worried that I would never get married, and so was I. Women who finished college without a husband were clearly in danger of spending their lives childless and alone.

What four boyfriends? A more accurate number was *zero* boyfriends.

Over the past four or five years, I had stopped sharing my inner landscape with my parents, telling myself (rightly or wrongly) that the range of their life experience did not give them the ability to show me a way to go down my road. My parents had been neighbors from the time they were ten years old, and at eighteen, they married, raising eight children over the next twenty-two years. For each of my parents, it was their first and only courtship. Several of my brothers' and sisters' marriages impressed me as dull at best and miserable at worst. The life of a housewife or a rural high school teacher threatened to be a trap for me and some unfortunate future husband. For me, the road to a happy relationship with a man seemed complex and, perhaps, unreachable.

Yet the pressure was there, not only from my father's expectations but from society's view of women my age—twenty-one—as potential spinsters. If we were to be fulfilled, we were told by professors, ministers, doctors, psychologists, advertisers, writers, and other women, we would find our purpose and happiness through being married. In the year I was graduating from college, Betty Friedan articulated the problem in her book *The Feminine Mystique*: "Over and over again, stories in women's magazines insist that women can know fulfillment only at the moment of giving birth to a child. They deny the years when she can no longer look forward to giving birth, even if she repeats the act over and over again. In the feminine mystique, there is no other way for a woman to dream of creation or of the future. There is no other way she can even dream about herself, except as her children's mother, her husband's wife."

I reviewed each of the dating situations I was in. Boyfriend 1, Jake, had returned from the Navy, but neither of us could, or wanted to, return to a serious relationship. Recently I had driven past a high school classmate's house on my way elsewhere and saw Jake's old green Pontiac parked in the street. Jake leaned against the car, smiling with the radiance of someone newly in love as he talked with my classmate's brothers. I was happy to see him that way, relieved that our relationship had died a natural death with little pain for either of us.

Boyfriend 2: In past months, I had dated Gus, taciturn son of an Iowa farmer, and, like me, a first-generation college student. His stoical, unexpressive manner felt familiar, much like the way I had been treated by my brothers. My attraction to him was probably that—his emotional distance felt familiar. But his actions told me that he was dating me as a possible conquest rather than someone he liked or admired. Our infrequent dates always ended with a tussle in the seat of his car on the dark country road leading to the farm. As I realized he did not understand or, probably, even know me, our midnight encounters felt more and more like angry battles of will. After one of these dates in which he felt he was "making progress," he sent me a cheap sentimental valentine. I furiously threw the card into the trash, promising myself to never see the chintzy wooden boor again.

Boyfriends 3 and 4: By summer, I was dating both of my singing partners, Travis and Greg. Travis was spending the summer at his childhood home three miles from me; Greg had gone to Omaha for a role in Summer Stock and seldom drove back to Maryville.

Travis and I had been playmates, classmates and singing partners for a very long time. In grade school, Travis and I organized "war games" at recess, masterminded the renovation of the coal shed into a mock general store, put tacks on classmates' seats to enliven a bleak February afternoon, and passed notes incessantly during class. We were bus seat buddies throughout high school. When we left the Wilcox country school the same year, we immersed ourselves in music. We sang Broadway duets at fairs, churches and concerts throughout the region, staring soulfully into each other's eyes the way Gordon McRae and Shirley Jones had in *Carousel* and *Oklahoma*. Travis had won a music scholarship to the University of Kansas but came back to Maryville during the summers to reluctantly help his father as little as possible on the farm.

My old friend now seemed interested in seeing me every day. He and Jonas, his best male friend—a fat, homely bachelor of forty—came by in Jonas's long white convertible to pick up me and Jonas's fiancée every day. We roamed the countryside, singing, dancing and socializing. Our home community observed with satisfaction: these two, Rosie and Travis, were going to be together and settle down at last, and they were best of friends with Jonas, that nice new minister. It troubled me that Travis didn't seem to want to spend time alone with me or kiss me or make any of the advances I'd come to expect. "He's shy," I thought, "because we were 'just friends' for so long."

Travis found out that I'd been dating Greg and said to me, "Greg's gay, you know. He meets other guys in the parking lot of Eddie's Market after it closes. I just thought you should know."

"I don't care about that."

I remembered Greg's passionate kisses and our intense romantic dates. I wasn't sure Travis wasn't talking about himself rather than Greg. Travis's lack of ardor and his fascination with his oily, sanctimonious friend confused me. My college classmates who had spent the last three years living away from their childhood homes would have figured it all out much earlier. Socially and emotionally, I was nearly in the same place I'd been three or four years earlier. In my loyal defense of Greg (or was it Travis?) I wasn't sure what I was standing in staunch support of, but it seemed that Travis's revelation was shocking and serious enough for me to heroically deny.

On a trip back from Omaha, Greg invited me to the drive-in movie.

"My mother doesn't approve of you because you're older than I am and not Catholic and my father's dying. I have to take care of Mom whenever I'm home. That's why I haven't been by. I'll see you after Summer Stock."

As much as I liked Greg, I wasn't upset, thinking that his mother could be right and that if her opinion meant more to him than I did, so be it. I knew, too, that Greg and Travis were looking at a professional horizon where I did not see myself going. They wanted to be professional singers more than anything, but I could not see myself achieving that.

Too short and freckled. I was not willing to work as a waitress and face rejection after rejection. There were many, too many, talented and beautiful sopranos out there.

Greg did not come back from Omaha but moved on to New York City, making his living as a prostitute at the "meat racks in Central Park," he told me years later.

As I packed for the move to Lawrence, I tried to sort out my now complicated relationship with Travis. How could he want to see me every single day and still not seem to have any passion for me except for one night when we shared a bottle of Chardonnay? I could not dismiss his need to always have Jonas (and his fiancée) with us, but I couldn't quite grasp what it all might mean. Jonas and Mindy got married that August and settled into life as a ministerial couple at the parsonage, five miles from where I lived.

At least he and Mindy aren't moving to Lawrence. Still—even if there were not the problem of Travis's notable lack of passion, there was his single-minded dream of singing professionally. I would not be going with him on that long journey.

By the end of August, Dad was reconciled to my going to graduate school, in part because I had dated Travis practically every day over the summer, and he thought the two of us were on our way to matrimony. My doting parents, now in their sixties, sent me off to KU with a '54 Chevrolet and a carload of potholders, old pans and dishes for settling into my first apartment. I had strained to get away from the farm and Maryville, but I grieved all the way to Savannah as I drove away from the life we'd shared together.

I thought I was driving to Lawrence alone, but that was an illusion. The people I had known in my life—my parents, brothers, Joy and Dolores, Greg, and Charlie—sat in the back seat, their legs dangling over the edge of my suitcase as if they were viewing me from the dock. They and every place that I had walked and every redolent scent of the lilac in our back yard I had smelled secreted themselves in my luggage, coming along with me.

After Savannah, the landscape subtly began to change as Highway 71 tracked closer to the Missouri River and its limestone bluffs. I had crossed an invisible boundary into less familiar land. I'd never return in spirit or mind, but I don't think any of us could have foretold the extent of that leaving.

The Great Divide

In August, Travis and I had driven to Lawrence, where he helped me find an apartment and introduced me to his friend Nancy, a voice major.

"How great it is going to be for us to be in the same university at last," he burbled.

Weeks went by at the university as I made the difficult transition from living on a farm with sixty-year-old parents to the teeming Civil Rights/early Hippie movements gustily sweeping into the halls of academe. Travis did not call or stop by. When I asked my new friend Nancy whether she had seen him, she said that she hadn't seen him since the beginning of school. Over the summer, I had recognized that there was no romantic future for Travis and me, but I did not expect my old friend to leave me completely on my own. To stave off my loneliness, I adopted a kitten and named him "Sunshine," my nickname for Travis from years past.

Finally, I drove to his apartment and was greeted by two slender, fashionable male roommates, their sunglasses perched on top of their curly heads. "Travis is not here right now."

They welcomed me in, showing off their high fashion white furnishings accented with "our cute new red phone."

"Do you want to leave a message for Travis?"

"No. No message."

As I absorbed the undeniable fact of Travis's deceit by omission, I drove back to my tiny free-standing house in one of the oldest sections of Lawrence. I had immediately loved the old brick streets, arching maple trees and occasional limestone houses of the neighborhood and now took comfort from them.

At Homecoming, I walked on Fraternity Row watching sleek leonine blond cheerleaders perch on the tops of the back seats of convertibles. Their drivers were inevitably the handsome future powerbrokers smugly secure in their privilege. I thought I had never seen such physically beautiful people—white corrected teeth flashing from faces still carrying the summer's poolside tan. They paraded down Fraternity Row on their way to the football game between the University of Missouri and the University of Kansas. Their mascot's name, the Jayhawk, said it all: a merger of two birds' names—the blue jay, a loud, quarrelsome thing known to harry smaller birds and rob their nests, and the sparrow hawk, a cunning, ferocious hunter. In an earlier depiction of the mascot, the Jayhawk had red legs, a direct reference to the Jayhawkers who had harried, robbed and murdered Missourians across the river in the lead-up to the Civil War. Coaches fired up their respective teams by reminding players of the enmity that had existed between the two states a hundred years before. Every fall, the bloody, tragic war was ritually re-enacted.

The bloodthirsty legacy and the smug Greek students in their convertibles stirred something in me that I could not name, perhaps Faulkner's sense that the past is never quite past and that it haunted us even as we moved beyond the middle of the twentieth century, perhaps a dawning of my recognition that the rage seeping up from the ground in my own home state shared this bloody Borderland history.

I continued walking to the student union, where I often spent my Saturday afternoons. The snack bar held rows of booths where graduate students gathered to read and find friends. That Saturday, none of the students I knew was there, so I felt melancholy as I read the densely printed annotations of *Hamlet* and heard the impassioned roars of fans in the football stadium blocks away. Glumly I remembered Thomas Mann stories I had recently read; he talked about the bright, blond sons and daughters of the light dancing heedlessly while others, dark and introspective, stood forever outside the circle looking on.

The size of the campus, as big as the town of Maryville, intimidated me, and I wondered how I would ever get to know anyone. My only friend was Nancy. We had little in common other than our mutual friend Travis, and she was a short-timer at the University. In her last year at KU, she was squandering her talent on an affair with a married fireman and was barely making her grades. She had agreed to be my piano accompanist when I practiced my voice lessons, but, as often as not, she didn't show up. Her mezzo-soprano voice flowed from her Teutonic six-foot frame as rich and smooth as chocolate sauce. When she sang German Lieder, her spellbound listeners thought perhaps they were in heaven, but I feared she wasn't going to take that voice beyond the nearest fire hydrant.

In my Classics course, I arranged study sessions with two other first-semester grad students. We formed an alliance out of desperation. As first-semester students, we came last in the registration for classes and had ended up with the worst and most difficult English professors. The Classics professor, himself ancient, sat in front of the sparsely en-rolled class and mumbled unintelligibly. We leaned forward, trying to catch a thread of thought. After class, we met to try to string together stray phrases and bits of sentences we had managed to capture in our notes. Together, we could sometimes figure out a line of thought. By Thanksgiving, we were an unlikely trio of friends: Caroline, a Jewish woman psychologically locked into her days at Wells College; Joseph, a prim product of Boston College, a Jesuit college for men; and me, from Nowhere.

Our circle of friends gradually expanded. Joseph had come to Kansas with two other Boston College graduates, Luke and Jordan. The two roommates could not have been more unlike Joseph. Jordan was annoyingly hyperactive, always wiggling, jiggling, and obses-sively talking about jazz or the women he had just laid or was current-ly planning to seduce. He was not attractive at all, picking his nose and breathing asthmatically between slurps of beer. I recognized him as a city version of my old boyfriend, Gus, and walked a big circle around him, having no interest in having my name added to his widely advertised conquest list. Jordan took my reticence as a challenge and showed up in my apartment every couple of weeks to try his luck and rifle through my phonograph albums, earmarking the ones he intended to pilfer later.

But Luke. Oh, Luke! I see him now, his big bearlike torso gyrating atop sturdy, slightly bowed legs as he bounced and swayed rhythmically to "I Wanna Hold Your Hand." His teeth flashed in an infectious grin as he sang the lyrics. He prided himself on his Italian Irish heritage and lived out his self-image as a rogue and poet. William Butler Yeats and Dylan Thomas rolled off his tongue while he chased after women and drank beer nightly at the Gaslight.

I was very taken with him, and he knew it. He dropped by my apartment from time to time to forage for food in my refrigerator and cupboards. He was always disappointed in what he found. I had no experience with junk food—no chips, no beer, no packaged sweets. To his horror, my cupboard was filled with ingredients—things I could cook with from scratch just as my mother had taught me.

When my kitchen yielded no food, he propositioned me, but knowing I had a crush on him, he followed up his query with a statement of honor. He had a former girlfriend in Boston that he couldn't get over.

"Cute as you are, that's where my heart is—still…if you feel like a quick tumble, it could be arranged." Our friendship developed on these terms: he would flirt, exhort me to get some food in the house and dance away.

As beginning graduate students, the five of us had been placed in the winnowing machine of the English faculty. The required course, "Bibliography," was designed to separate the wheat from the chaff, the diligent and prepared from the slackers and unprepared. Only Joseph and I spent any time studying, and my academic preparation for graduate work was dismal, so the survival of our group of five did not look promising. At mid-term, I got a "C" with a letter ordering me to meet with the Graduate School Dean. My friends got the same summons, but none of us talked about it. We skulked into our appointments. The stern-faced dean kept us standing before him.

"In this graduate school, if you get two C grades, you are out. Raise your grades or face the consequences. You may not be graduate school material."

I doubled down on the hours I spent in the library studying "quartos" and "folios" and "leaves" of rare books and raised my grade in the odious course. My prospects in the other classes were better. When I walked out of my eighteenth-century poetry class with an "A" paper in hand, Luke caught up with me.

"How did you do that?" he asked incredulously. In his own hand, he held his "B" paper, stung to be outdone by his country bumpkin friend.

The five of us underwent the winnowing process in another way. We were members of a lesser class within the social stratification of academe from the get-go. We did not graduate from prestigious Ivy League or Big 10 schools; we did not earn prestigious national scholarship competitions. We had come through our undergraduate years from colleges such as Boston College, founded by Jesuits to serve the Irish working class, and Northwest, a teacher's college in a remote corner of Missouri. Wells College produced well-prepared liberal arts graduates, but my brilliant friend had not applied herself. The insularity of her Jewish upbringing in a New Jersey suburb and her cosseted existence in the small private women's college on the shores of Lake Cayuga rendered her as culturally ill-prepared for the large Midwestern university as I was. She had come to KU with no clear idea of what she wanted from graduate study, her undergrad days having been focused primarily on chocolate treats, sleeping late and using her lively mind to play dormitory pranks.

The English graduate students who came from the better schools, with more prestigious academic records, and, in most cases, much greater wealth, had assistantships, fellowships and offices. In the office setting, they hobnobbed with their professors from the beginning and formed their friendships and networks in those offices. Absorbed in their own career goals and friendships, they were oblivious of the fringe first-year grad students they passed in the halls on their way to cozy seminars of twelve. They had built-in social support systems and, by and large, were focused, self-disciplined, politically savvy scholars with their sights set on plum academic positions after finishing their PhDs. It was easy for professors to see themselves in these students, and the teachers routinely handed out invitations to cocktail parties and job notices at prestigious universities. If one of us fringe academics appeared at their office doors, they looked quizzically at us over the tops of their glasses, wondering who we were. If any of us survived to the doctoral level, they would learn our names then.

On the Friday afternoon before Thanksgiving, I trudged up Mount Oread to my eighteenth-century poetry class in the venerable, structurally unsound Fraser Hall. The wobbling walnut banister and worn oak stairs creaked and groaned as dozens of students climbed to their classes on the upper floors of the building. The line of ascending students came to a standstill. Unmoving masses of people filled the halls above us. We stood on the staircase trying to hear what some authoritative voice in the hall was saying. Telegraph-style, the message began to filter down: Kennedy had been assassinated. We stood there, numb and silent, not knowing what to do. It only dawned on me later that I heard about the death of my generation's symbol of hope and social justice in that building. Fraser Hall, built by Lawrence's abolitionist settlers just eleven years after the close of the Civil War, stood on the steep hill above Lawrence as an emblem of enlightenment.

Crying and talking in hushed tones to our classmates, we drifted into our classrooms. Professor Taylor, pale and shaken, sat at the front of the class. Finally, he opened the book in front of him. Dipping into a volume written a century before the poets we were studying, he read from poems of John Donne, his voice barely audible as tears dropped on the page.

Holy Sonnets: Death, be not proud
by John Donne

Death, be not proud, though some have called thee
Mighty and dreadful, for thou art not so;

> For those whom thou think'st thou dost overthrow
> Die not, poor Death, nor yet canst thou kill me.
> From rest and sleep, which but thy pictures be,
> Much pleasure; then from thee much more must flow,
> And soonest our best men with thee do go,
> Rest of their bones, and soul's delivery.
> Thou art slave to fate, chance, kings, and desperate men,
> And dost with poison, war, and sickness dwell,
> And poppy or charms can make us sleep as well
> And better than thy stroke; why swell'st thou then?
> One short sleep past, we wake eternally
> And death shall be no more; Death, thou shalt die.

Most of us had plans to go home for Thanksgiving and went our stunned, sad ways that afternoon. In the following days, I watched the black and white images of the president lying in state, the caisson rumbling down Pennsylvania Avenue, his black-veiled widow and little John and Caroline at grave's edge.

A call came in for me from Nancy, my vocal accompanist.

"Will you be the bride's maid at my wedding?" she asked, her voice tinsel.

"Wedding?"

"Oh yes, I am marrying my boyfriend here in Kansas City at Christmas time. You'll need to wear a long, dark green velvet dress because it's a holiday wedding."

I had never heard of this boyfriend in Kansas City—all I had heard about were the encounters with her fireman lover during his many long afternoons off duty. Mom and I began to plan the sewing and fitting of the velvet dress I couldn't afford out of my meager graduate student budget. It was going to be simple and elegant, something like the dresses worn by Jacqueline Kennedy.

Between Thanksgiving and Christmas, Nancy's fiancée must have done his math. The five-month baby bulge Nancy now had could not be containing his baby. Early in the morning on the last day of

1963, Nancy called again. "The wedding is off," she said through her blanket of sobs.

"I am going to a home for unwed mothers to have the baby and put it up for adoption."

No more fireman, no more lieder, no more adoring affluent parents parading her talent before the congregation at their suburban church, no degree. Oh, and no more baby.

Before I left the farm to return to campus, I folded the velvet gown in tissue paper and put it in the cedar chest. It seemed to have been conceived of a century ago rather than when Kennedy was shot less than six weeks earlier. I stored the elegant green dress away along with the innocence I had in 1963, the world of simple melodic songs, and the illusion of making a joyful unimpeded leap into a predictable bright future.

I continued to scratch away at course requirements, but my interests lay with my ongoing struggle to figure out how to traverse the perilous terrain I walked on and to plug holes in my woeful academic background. I discovered that an introductory art history course was taught in a lecture hall holding over two hundred students and that the lecturers discussed giant images of immortal artworks they displayed on a screen. I inched my way into the lecture hall and sat down, hoping to steal in and hear every lecture. It was easy to merge with the other students unnoticed. I attended all lectures and bought the hugely expensive text, *Janson's History of Art*. The pages opened to a whole new world of beauty. I vowed I would go to Europe and see those paintings and sculptures one day.

At about that time, I began dating Tad, the only son of a newspaper editor in Wellington, Kansas. One of the fringe master's degree students, he had been at KU throughout his undergraduate years, and after a forced stint in the Army, he returned to campus and began his master's degree coursework. He relished telling the story of how he had outfoxed the Army after he was drafted and ordered to report for duty. Having no interest in serving as a target in Viet Nam, Tad carefully chose answers to questions on the Army aptitude tests. His answers disqualified him from any tasks remotely related to weapons, driving or any other skill pointing to combat duty. His answers instead indicated that he could play the French horn in the Army band. The Army band director soon figured out that Tad could play only the two songs he'd learned in ninth-grade band and had Tad transferred to the army post office. Tad spent his military time sitting behind the mail counter reading novels and chewing Red Man Tobacco.

His time reading novels was well spent. He had read the works of authors I'd never heard of—Norman Mailer, Jean Genet, and Ken Kesey—and he passed these books and issues of *I. F. Stone's Weekly* on to me after he'd read them. I. F. Stone had been drummed out of his job at a major newspaper during the McCarthy era and subsequently turned to publishing a punctiliously documented bi-weekly newsletter covering Washington, DC.

Stone's documentation of the escalation of the war in Viet Nam shocked me into recognizing what was happening there.

Special 8-Page Issue Documenting The Tonkin Gulf Fraud

McNamara and The Right to Lie

"The Secretary . . . has kept secret important communications from the task force that indicated doubt about the reported attack on Aug. 4. . . . Secretary McNamara's statement is a classic example of selective declassification. . . . Security classification is intended to protect the nation from an enemy, not . . . one branch of government against another or the public, nor to protect the American people from knowledge of mistakes. I do not accept as valid the view of Mr. Arthur Sylvester, the former press officer of the Pentagon, that the Government has a right to lie to the people of this country."

—Sen. Fulbright of Senate Foreign Relations Feb. 21

I. F. Stone's Weekly

Now Published Bi-Weekly

VOL. XVI, NO. 5   MARCH 4, 1968   WASHINGTON, D. C.   20 CENTS

My mind exploded with the dark, random, absurd visions laid before me. Soon I was drawn into Tad's circle of friends, other alienated, dark-humored Kansas graduates. We gathered in his friend Clay's apartment almost every night, listening to John Coltrane, Bessie Smith, Charlie Mingus or Wolfman Jack, telling stories of past anti-social antics and smoking "ditch weed." There were two or three women in the group besides me, but none of us made any effort to befriend each other—our sole function in the group was to serve as an accessory to the men spinning tales for each other.

Alison was Aaron's soul mate, and the couple embodied all the romantic and sexual fantasies of the group. The women envied Aaron's laid-back companionable affection for Alison and marveled at Aaron's Adonis beauty. The men carefully jockeyed to position themselves directly across from where Alison sat cross-legged in our circle. She wore a short mini-skirt above-knee socks and sturdy walking shoes, carefully cultivating a sex-laced earth mother image straight out of Slavic sculpture. Both she and Aaron pretended not to know that the men in the group could not concentrate on anything but the exposed crotch of her panties, but both basked in the attention she drew. The men smoked pot, nodded to the music, and drooled with desire.

At the time, I did not think about the way the women in the group did not interact with each other. I had grown accustomed to seeing almost exclusively male faces at the lectern in front of me in classes and in the students' chairs beside me. The luminaries we studied were also men. Women didn't do anything but serve as the subjects of men's sexual longings and romantic fantasies unless they were their mothers, and then they were harridans to be avoided. Women were the blank canvases on which the men painted self-absorbed images of themselves.

Tad began to move on to other women and other drugs. I could not fill the dark abyss inside him, and he could not commit to anyone or anything. We both stayed in the circle, edging around each other with a mixture of friendship and hostility. Tad, his friend Clay, and I walked down dark brick streets on summer nights, each drinking from a quart-sized bottle of beer. We stood on the banks of the Kansas River listening to frogs and locusts, watching rotting pieces of logs float down the muddy river, and breathing in the hot, humid air that cloaked the moon. We sometimes ducked into "Okie bars" to listen to Johnny Cash on the jukeboxes placed at the ends of the ratty plastic booths. Clay and Tad, both men of small stature, talked about having to fight their ways out of the bar after defending me from drunken rednecks. That never happened, but they liked imagining it.

I walked across campus on a late spring day wondering how I could pay for school in the coming year. My one-year scholarship would soon expire. To pay my rent, I was going to manage the apartments in a run-down nineteenth-century house on Ohio Street, so I was partway to covering my expenses.

One of my professors passed me on the sidewalk then suddenly turned around and said, "Do you want a job?" he asked.

His federal grant to establish an English as a Foreign Language Program (as such programs were then called) had just come through. I immediately signed on to conduct "drill and practice" sessions and teach intermediate grammar to thirty Middle Eastern students.

My professor had been instrumental in establishing a descriptive linguistic approach to language learning at the University of Michigan to prepare translators during World War II. Now the method was applied to our program at KU, part of the national effort to establish the US as the central influence on the oil-rich Arab language countries. The program thrust me into the current linguistic thinking of the time and contact with people from vastly different cultures. It was the beginning of yet another cognitive and cultural revolution for me.

No one thought to tell me how I should dress for the class, so I wore sleeveless summer dresses left over from my undergraduate days. As I stood before my grammar class of thirty men from Egypt and the United Arab Emirates, I was annoyed at how little attention they paid to the examples on the board.

Why were they bothering to be here?

Gradually I realized that rather than staring out the window at the heat waves simmering outside, they were staring fixedly at my armpits and waiting for me to lift my arms to point out a grammatical feature on the blackboard. I was performing what, for them, must have been a girly peep show! Little by little, the students and I discovered the edges where our cultures bumped unhappily against each other. We moved through the summer together in a march toward Grammar III in the fall semester.

The house I moved to was quiet that summer, the residents on the floor above me chipping away at course requirements by day and climbing through a window at night to sit on the flat roof, drink a beer and smoke pot. Occasionally anti-war activists from Berkeley or New York University crashed on our sagging couches for a few nights as they traveled across the country from university to university. As the smokers finished their joints, they threw them to the ground below and sat perched on their haunches, scrawny knees drawn up to their chests, and looked out on the brick streets below, waiting for something to happen.

"Luke's having a party at his place," Tad said to me one hot afternoon.

We drove to the spreading old Victorian house where he and Jordan had a second-floor apartment. Music blasted loudly through the open windows and down the stairs. Luke and Jordan had already begun putting down cans of beer, and they immediately reached into a cooler to ply a few other guests and us with beer.

Luke was unusually frenetic, holding a can of beer and dancing in the middle of the floor to Buddy Holly.

"I brought you here to tell you I'm going to die."

We stood in a circle around him, unsure of what was happening and of how to respond. His vibrancy, youth and legendary love of conning people made us hesitant to believe him.

"For real. I have lymphoma and I have six months to live. It's the cancer that kills young people."

We gasped.

"Dance! No tears. We have to live now!"

Buddy Holly's "That'll be the day" began to play, and Luke immediately began to sing and dance to it.

> *Well that'll be the day, when you say good-bye,*
>
> *Yes, that'll be the day when you make me cry*
>
> *You say you're gonna leave, you know it's a lie…*

Falteringly we joined in, caught up in Luke's intensity until Buddy hit that terrible line, "Cause that'll be the day when I die!" Our voices stumbled and faded into silence—even Luke's.

The party was over. We left quietly in ones and twos, saying goodbye to Luke as he sat quietly now in a corner chair. I sank down in the seat of Tad's car and began to sob.

"I'm so sorry. I can't stop."

"That's okay. I hope someday someone will cry for me."

We didn't hear much from Luke over the next months. He enrolled in classes but was mostly absent from them. He didn't want to talk about the lymphoma and withdrew into himself.

On a cold November night, a couple of hours after midnight, he knocked at my door. He was pale and drawn, cold drops of sweat dripping at his hairline.

"Can you just hold me?" he asked.

I snuggled against him in my bed, any thoughts of joking propositions set aside. He lay on his side, his body in a cold sweat. We lay together until dawn, a river of tears flooding our pillows.

"I have to go home."

"Do you want me to drive you? Do you want your family to come get you?"

"No, I want to do this myself. Drive myself home."

I wrote a check to pay for his way home and watched him drive down between the bare trees lining Ohio Street like splintered masts in an abandoned harbor. His old white Buick glided down the street, a ship leaving the harbor to cast itself into the cold gray fog.

After Luke was gone, the threads binding the circle of friends began to fray. We were preparing to leave Lawrence over the next few months, each on to the sequel of our KU act. Some were going East for doctorates, and some were drifting West to Haight-Ashbury in an LSD haze. Tad was looking around for a low-challenge doctoral program at KU that would enable him to maintain his lifestyle of beer, pot and younger women. I never knew, until fifty years later, thanks to the internet, that he was more deeply into the drug scene than I thought—even to the point of selling the stuff.

In an interview with Jim McCrary, the poet talks about Tad and those years in Lawrence: "I fell in with the free-wheeling literati at the Abingdon Bookshop, forming lasting friendships with the likes of *Grist* publisher John Fowler and writers Charles Plymell and George Kimball, and later with William S. Burroughs, S. Clay Wilson and Allen Ginsberg... I wrote a short story illustrating the life of proto-Hippies in Lawrence, which was published in the *Evergreen Review*."

In talking about the Rock Chalk Café: "Ahh...the Chalk... we used to call it. Was certainly a very important spot in Lawrence for a few years. At the end of a block on top of a hill looking over the Kansas River valley. At the other end of the block, was the Gaslight Tavern, which was another beer and hamburger joint where college professors and college football players and hippies all hung out together... Mostly, in the beginning, it was a place to go for folks who didn't fit in at the downtown college or farmer bars. Was before the summer of love, 1965 or so... People called each other "freaks" then...not hippies or beats. We discovered LSD...in fact me and a guy named Tad Hoff went to Chicago and bought a big bag of purple acid and brought it back and distributed it around town. Later the hippy thing came, and the Chalk was the place to go. There were a lot of folks who came up from Wichita to Lawrence. Artists, writers and just plain strange like Tad

Hoff who was a kind of crazy but smart guy who took a lot
of drugs and was kind of a shaman."

–Jim McCrary in Keep the Blues Alive-Blues GR blog,
posted by Michalis Limnios BLUES@GREECE, July 28,
2013, Accessed March 29, 2014

Caroline planned to marry a doctoral student and find a circle
to sit in where she could continue to spin her tales of days at Wells
College. She had made a fine art of not studying a practice honed to
perfection in her days at Wells. One day I dropped by her apartment
and, when I knocked, she refused to come to the door, though I knew
she was inside. It was the week before finals, so I concluded that she
was cramming for her exams.

"Carrie, I know you're studying in there," I called through the
door. When there was no answer, I left.

The next time she saw me, she said, "You know that day you
came by and said I was studying? I wasn't. I was sleeping."

"How are you doing this?" I asked.

"You just put out the B. S. I get *CliffsNotes* for works in the literary period for the class, and I make an essay of the notes. It works
every time. It's all bullshit."

At the nightly circle, she crowed in triumph over the "A" grades
she raked in as a result of the few hours a semester spent summarizing the *CliffsNotes*, couching the distilled critical outlines in elegant
rhetoric. The professors were carried away on the paper's wings. In
over five years of "work" as an English major at both Wells and KU,
she was never caught elegantly summarizing "the Cliffs" and she
continued embracing her Animal House cynicism, as far as I know,
forever.

I became disenchanted with the nightly gathering of the circle. I
was on the fringe of the fringe, a cautionary voice that I, for once, listened to telling me to stay away from the drugs tearing at my friends'
cores. The group was in a rut, doing and saying the same thing every
night and finding their repetitive tales endlessly profound or funny. I
needed to move on.

After reading *Women in Love* and D. H. Lawrence's early poems, I became interested in his work, and Tad advised me to approach Dr. Crawford, the department specialist in twentieth-century literature.

"He is seldom on campus and won't bother you. He's just come off his extra-marital affair with the English Department's graduate student goddess, Juliette, and he's sitting by the pool at his house drinking whiskey—lots of it."

Crawford was, indeed, sitting by his pool and coming to campus as little as possible. He had never met me, but he agreed to be my thesis advisor. I toiled away at my thesis, never finding him in his office and never actually seeing his face. I left my thesis outline in his mailbox and got a note approving my topic sometime after.

I was depressed and resigned to the grinding isolation I faced as I crawled through the final steps toward the degree. I was saddened by Luke's death, the sorry ending to my recent romances, the drug-induced unraveling of friends' minds and my struggle to survive both academically and personally. I no longer believed in much of anything; most of all, I did not believe in myself. My path toward adulthood these past two years had been covered over with kudzu vines that threatened to entwine me in their grip and throw me to the ground. The struggle had taken a toll. I feared that I would fail my oral exams scheduled for late in the summer and that Crawford would wreak havoc with my thesis if ever I got it finished. A more overarching anxiety was that I had no idea what could become of me next.

Master's degree candidates were required to read and prepare to discuss the one hundred literary works on the orals reading list. It didn't matter whether we had taken graduate-level courses in all the centuries and genres represented on the list; we were responsible for being able to comment, hopefully intelligently, on them all. I doggedly began to march through the list and write my thesis.

In late May, I dropped the thesis off at Crawford's house, smelling his boozy breath as he cracked open the high gate to his deck to receive the sheaf of paper. A few days later, he returned the draft through campus mail marked "approved" with the single comment, "Solid work. Your writing style took on D. H. Lawrence's in that last chapter." That last offhand sentence did not make me happy. I had become thoroughly sick of D. H. Lawrence as I wrote about his later years. His abstract, self-worshipping descriptions of his wife Frieda and other women were about as accurate as a giraffe's description of a nun's underpants. I looked at the draft.

Yes, my last chapter had the abstract, wind-blown style of Lawrence's later works, but, hell, I didn't care. I took the approval and immediately sent the draft to my niece in Missouri to type. We had made a deal that I would buy her a new Smith-Corona typewriter to take to college if she would type my thesis. Seeing the end of my time in Lawrence coming to an end, I began sending out job applications and preparing for orals.

I read joylessly in those months, occasionally hanging out with my friend Tanya. She and I attended a post-Civil Rights demonstration party in an old house down the street. Dozens and dozens of students from the day's march in Topeka squeezed up the stairs to the hosts' apartment. Nobody knew these people—we had just heard that there was a big loud party there.

Tanya and I didn't know anyone at the party, and we made our way through the crowded rooms, soon becoming separated. A tall thin man sat alone in the alcove of a bay window, looking out over the street. I stood by him, and we began to talk.

"Do you know anyone here?" I asked.

"No. I've just moved here from Topeka."

Our talk drifted to books we'd read, writers we liked, our views on the Viet Nam War. When I saw Tanya across the room, I joined her and we left, hoping to get out before the dangerously over-crowded apartment collapsed into the floor below. When she and I were at the Gaslight a week or so later, Adam, the tall, thin man, joined us at our table.

He wasn't like the others, and I was drawn to his shy smile. As he told Tanya and me of his life as a young writer in Paris, I began to fall in love with the idea of being part of a life like that—living in a little hotel on the Left Bank, sipping coffee and watching Parisians pass by, meeting people like James Baldwin or Anthony Quinn at

Les Deux Magots, and browsing for English language books from Shakespeare's. In his tweed sport jacket with patches at the elbow, he didn't look much like the writers he'd hung out with in Paris, cadaverous William Burroughs, antic bearded Ginsburg, or frenetic Gregory Corso.

The crabapple trees were bursting with pink blossoms cascading over the old brick sidewalks where we walked on sunny afternoons. He brought strawberries and camembert for intimate little picnics. I was troubled by some of his mannerisms and perceptions of people and events, but I had become so used to the dark, absurd visions of my fringe friends that Adam didn't seem that much different from them. Lonely, depressed, anxious about the future and distancing myself from my recent past, I turned off my alarm bells.

Romance or not, the day arrived that I was to show up on a Saturday morning for my orals. My steps echoed in the cavernous open space; the halls were empty except for a student desk placed—ominously it seemed to me—by itself outside a classroom door. Three professors sat inside, two of whom I had never met. They sat in a circle of student desks they had arranged with an empty one waiting for me. They seemed sleepy and grumpy on that weekend morning, having been assigned the tedious task of putting the current crop of master's degree candidates through their paces. Clearly, they would rather have been sitting at home in their bathrobes and drinking a leisurely cup of coffee.

They began their list of questions without interest. I didn't think the exam was going well because of their lack of eye contact, and I was filled with dread and despair that so much of my future rested on their assessment. A professor asked a desultory question about *The Snows of Kilimanjaro* involving the contrast between the two men in the story and the purpose of that contrast.

Before I could stop myself, I heard my voice coming from a place inside me that I almost didn't recognize. My Jell-O pie-throwing self was still alive in there somewhere. I looked at the professor and said, "Actually, there were three men in the story," and I elaborated then on their contrasting positions in the story. The professor looked up sharply and straightened in his seat, suddenly awake, and the exam took on a new, brisker tone that I wasn't sure how to interpret.

As I awaited the professors' verdict in the dim, vacant hallway outside the classroom, I thought, "I've done it now." Why didn't I answer that question and the ones to follow in a more carefully diplomatic way? My pent-up anger at months, no years, of self-absorbed professors looking over the tops of their students' heads—particularly those of women students—had finally boiled over. They were asking me to perform when they had done nothing to coach me or encourage my success. I resented their indifferent postures and that they, who had never even known my name, had so much power.

Professor Taylor strode jauntily through the classroom door.

"You did brilliantly. Where have you been? I don't think I've ever seen you before."

Postcards from Points of Reckoning

Baby Boomers were pouring into Illinois State University and I, needing a job by fall, responded to the university's invitation for an interview. I rode through the night on a Trailways bus from Lawrence to St. Louis, tossing, turning and finally settling on my side in the seat to sleep a few hours. I woke up as the bus pulled into the dirty, derelict St. Louis bus terminal, suddenly aware that the passenger in the seat next to me had been fondling my backside for some time. He refused to look at me, scuttling off into the seven a.m. crowds in the dimly lit bus station.

I had worn my jeans on the bus but now changed clothes in the filthy restroom of the terminal. I caught my connection to Normal, Illinois, looking fresh, professional and very young in a trim brown tweed summer suit and two-and-a-half-inch bone-colored heels. The department chairman and his wife met me at the bus stop, never suspecting that they were looking at a near-miss "Freak," as post-Beatnik/pre-Hippies called themselves—and they would have cared, had they known.

I was hired to teach four sections of freshman composition to the blond farm kids populating the newly built, bland high-rise dorms at the edge of campus. As I filled out my employment papers, I looked at the attached Loyalty Oath in some bewilderment. What was this Joe McCarthy era hold-over supposed to accomplish? Surely if I were a Communist infiltrator intent on overthrowing the government, I would be smart enough not to bring attention to myself by refusing to sign the oath. A voice from *The Wizard of Oz* chanted inside my head, "Dorothy, you're not in Kansas anymore."

My transformation from a freaky graduate student into a beginning regional university instructor was not seamless, especially because I brought Adam with me to Normal. In moving from a politically active university campus to a place called *Normal*, it would have been a logical time for me to tell Adam that we needed to split up. There was no way that a man like Adam was going to fit into Normal, Illinois, and, too, I had begun to wonder about several of his habits and stories he told me about his past life. Prior to moving to Lawrence, he had been a long-time resident at Menninger's Clinic in Topeka—schizophrenia, he said. I thought many of his alienated, sensitive perspectives came from his having lived in Paris in his teens amongst the expat writers on the Left Bank. His formative years had been spent immersing himself in literature and lifestyles of the counterculture. In those times, it was hard for a romantic, imaginative English major like me to distinguish between an anti-hero and a madman. Either way, the staid agricultural community surrounding the regional university at Normal had never seen anything like him, and he hated the place at first sight, and the people there likely feared and disliked him, too.

My head filled with stories of artists living on the edge in France or returning to the land to sustain their creativity. I did not listen to the doubts crowding in at the edges of my mind. I did not know how to turn away the only man who ever wanted or needed to follow me anywhere. I heard strong voices of cultural expectation telling me I could end up being "an Old Maid Schoolteacher." I was, after all, approaching the age of twenty-three, which in 1966 was considered dangerously close to spinsterhood.

On a dreary September day, I left campus and returned to my apartment, changing into the brown tweed suit I'd worn for my interview a few weeks earlier. The three-day waiting period between getting a marriage license and having the marriage ceremony performed had passed. When we arrived at the McLean County Courthouse to meet the presiding judge, a clerk told us that we had to wait for him because a murder trial was taking longer than expected.

We stood on the dirty marble steps leading up to the courthouse. The heat and humidity still hovered over the flat Illinois landscape by the clouds lowering over our heads. An hour passed. Adam wandered on the courthouse grounds, gloomy and uncommunicative. I found a place to sit among the smashed cigarette butts on the steps and wilted in the heat. "Don't do this," my inner voice pleaded.

"I have to. I promised," a different inner voice said.

I sat on the steps near tears, dejected and confused. The clerk emerged from the courthouse.

"The judge is ready now," she said. "But you have to have two witnesses. Where are your witnesses?"

When we told her we didn't know we had to have witnesses and knew no one in the city, she turned impatiently and returned inside. A few minutes later, she came back. "I've found two people who will be your witnesses. They were part of the murder trial, but they'll wait for you to get married."

A hard-faced woman in her fifties stood sullenly at the door to the judge's chambers. Her bleached, frizzy blond hair framed her ruddy, lined face. She stared sideways rather than look at the beefy red-faced man beside her, his beer belly straining the buttons of his blue plaid shirt. The hefty pair stood without speaking at our sides and gazed around the room while the over-tired judge rattled through the marriage ceremony. Then the three left, vanishing through the chamber doors and on to their lives, whatever they were.

One thing I had learned from Adam was to appreciate continental foods—escargots, beef burgundy and Caesar salad, so to celebrate our marriage, Adam and I ate at The Terrace, the best restaurant in town that night, and planned ways we could stockpile money to go live in Paris. We would live on Adam's trust fund money and the proceeds from Adam's writing. What would I do? I'd be a writer's wife, I imagined, meeting fascinating people, savoring life in beautiful Paris, and reading the cornucopia of books inviting me to pick them up. Adam would publish stories in *The Evergreen Review* or *The Paris Review* and eventually write a novel rivaling Norman Mailer's, we thought.

When we told our families about our marriage, neither was happy. The summer before, Adam and I had driven to Santa Fe to see his sister Melissa. She watched me coldly as we sipped Snow on the Mountain cocktails at the storied Pink Adobe. When I got up to go to the bathroom, I heard her hiss at Adam, "You aren't going to marry *her*, are you?" She had taken in my wholesome Midwestern looks, unable to be disguised by ethnic beads and jeans, and determined that I was a sweet, naïve, conventional girl totally unsuited by class and rural background for Adam. The comment was my second exposure of the day to the social class Adam came from. Earlier in the day, a family friend invited Adam and me to her spacious original adobe. As she sat languidly on a deck chair, she eyed me.

"Her hair reminds me of Shamrock, my Irish Setter's," she said, combing her long turquoise studded fingers through the dog's hair. She continued talking to Adam, coolly ignoring me as if I were one of the pieces of pottery edging the patio.

We took the train to visit Adam's grandmother Leona, a silver-haired widow of a millionaire businessman in western Kansas. As Santa Fe Railroad's long svelte Silver Chief pulled into the station in Hutchinson, Kansas, at midnight, she was waiting for us. Despite the heat, the eighty-six-year-old woman wore an elaborately rhinestone-studded purple sweater and dyed-to-match skirt. She tottered stiffly on high heels to her Cadillac; a mink fur draped around her heavily powdered neck. She was as concerned about the marriage as Adam's sister, but from an entirely different perspective. She had raised Adam and his sister following their parents' divorce and their mother's crippling multiple sclerosis. The two were bright, troubled teenagers, and when Adam became unmanageable in junior high school, his grandmother sent him to a military academy hoping "to straighten him out." The military school experience was disastrous. Adam suffered a mental breakdown and was committed to a mental health facility for teenagers. From that time on, he had been in and out of mental institutions.

Leona understood, more than anyone else, that Adam could not function as a husband or father. She didn't tell me any of this, of course, and—to be fair—I didn't ask. I believed all of Adam's horror stories about her heartless treatment of him, wanting to see him as a misunderstood artist. She accepted me as best she could but must have known all along that, if I stayed with Adam, my role would be more that of caretaker than wife. She may even have hoped that I could relieve her of some of the burden of trying to cope with his illness and his mother's invalidism. I often felt like "the hired girl" in her presence.

Our family visits included a drive to my parents' farm that summer. They regarded the strange bird I had brought home and were terrified that I would marry him. As Adam and my parents tried to interact, they could not find any topic that could be sustained for more than five minutes. Nervous and shy, he retreated to his bedroom upstairs, claiming he had to do some writing. He sat on the edge of the bed for hours, rocking and staring at the wall. He did not know how to play any board games or cards, knew nothing of farming or gardening, and looked pallid and alien in his white long-sleeved shirt and black slacks. They, of course, were edgy and awkward, glancing nervously at each other if he made any references to having lived abroad or not having a job but a trust fund allotment. Years later, my brother Max told me that after I phoned my mother to tell her I was marrying Adam, she hoed her garden and wept for several days, just as she had done when her sons went to war.

From the few academic parties we attended in Normal to Adam's walks across campus, his tall crow-like figure clad in a long black over-coat, we were soon identified as somehow not being "standard issue." We might as well have had labels pasted to our foreheads: MISFITS; other unfortunately placed teachers at the college sought us out. In the few months we were in Normal, our contacts with them were brief and irregular. The music teacher who spent his time building harpsichords vanished after he visited while I was at work, his red silk bikini briefs for a lakeside picnic coming to naught. Art Blankenship, who shared an office with me in our English instructor office suite, faded from sight too after Adam walked in on him just as Art came up behind me to caress my back.

"You fascinate me," he had been saying. "Every day, you come to the office in a different costume. Who are you?"

His observation was apt: one day, I would wear a crisp navy blue and white suit and heels with my hair twisted in a French roll. The next day I might have on a long peasant skirt and ethnic beads around my neck, my hair hanging wildly to my collarbones. I had no more idea who I was than he did. I tried on different identities, trying to have my life fit both traditional academic norms and counterculture patterns. I was conducting my life the same way, on one hand trying to fill the role of wife and breadwinner, and, on the other, trying to retain the artsy "freak" identity that had begun to form at KU.

We formed the closest acquaintance with an art professor, Mel McBride, and his wife, who had that year moved to Normal from New York City. They were even more ill-suited to Illinois State than we were: they were life-long New Yorkers, politically active in Civil Rights and anti-war causes, Jewish, and experimental abstract painters. In September, an effort to mobilize groups to protest the United States' involvement in the Viet Nam War began at Illinois State when a group organizer came to campus that fall from the West Coast. Mel, six to eight young male students and I, the only woman, met in a small classroom to talk about organizing local protests.

Relishing their feeling of potency, the young men leaned intensely into the discussion, their voices vying for dominance. It was a familiar, tedious scenario. I hadn't heard of the organization yet, but in June, a group of women in Washington, DC, fed up with sitting on the sidelines of Civil Rights and Viet Nam protest strategy sessions, had formed the National Organization for Women. Less than a year later, bright, college-educated women would begin holding consciousness-raising meetings in New York and Chicago, finally giving a voice to their unwillingness to be ignored, voiced over and held down. While I agreed to support the anti-war effort, I declined to sign the membership roster; my focus was already on Adam's and my plan to leave for France the following summer. I had read that there were FBI agents infiltrating some of these groups to identify potential radicals and, with an eye to getting a passport with no problem, I wanted to stay in the background.

On a cold, windy day in January, I looked out my office window to see Adam and Mel standing alone on the campus commons holding protest placards up as students and teachers, avoiding eye contact, hurried past. President Lyndon Johnson had announced that the United States would stay in Viet Nam until the "Communist Aggression" there had ended; by January 18, the number of US troops in Viet Nam totaled 190,000. The brash young men of the planning meeting were nowhere in sight. Mel and Adam were a lonely pair, and they soon disappeared, their statement made and, seemingly, ignored in the smug, well-meaning land of Normal, Illinois. We rode the train to Chicago for the March 26, 1966, International Day of Protest, joining thousands of Americans who marched through their city streets that day. A great deal of momentum in the anti-war movement had occurred by then, with public support for the war declining from 52 percent to 37 percent by the end of 1965, but some of that 37 percent stood lining the streets screaming "Commie!" and "traitor" as we marched. We got through the day without getting our heads bashed in but felt the intensity of the anger directed at us and recognized the march as a precursor to the violent confrontations that would inevitably come. Leaving the country was looking better than ever.

A great deal of my attraction to Adam was that he had traveled across the country and in Europe; I eagerly embraced the prospect of sailing to Europe in the coming summer. His travels were not the road trips I knew as a child with my parents where we drove all day, stopping at diners and filling stations on the highway, taking in historic and scenic places of interest and cramming ourselves into cheap tourist cottages. His experience embraced luxurious hotels, air travel, cocktails, and dinner in the dining car of a cross-country train, lengthy stays in Santa Fe resorts and beat hotels in Greenwich Village and living in Paris. I wanted the adventure, social class, and intellectual worlds that he could take me to.

We boarded the *T. S. Bremen* in New York in early July.

We had booked passage at the cheapest rate possible and so found ourselves wedged into a tiny cabin on the bottom passenger level. The air was close and hot. No one knew to tell me that to avoid seasickness, I needed to breathe in fresh air and move about the ship, so on the first night of the six-day voyage, I put myself to bed in the narrow berth as the ship left the harbor. By the middle of the night, I was sick, by the next morning, even sicker. I lay in my berth as still as I could while Adam roamed around the ship. On the second day of the voyage, I forced myself to weave dizzily down the corridor to the dining room. The smell of heavily sauced continental food blasted my way. Even the economy class dining area was beautifully appointed with white linen tablecloths and heavy flatware. The menu was elegantly printed, and the waiters stood deferentially at our sides to take our orders, but the words undulated before my eyes. I ate soup but groped my way back to the cabin for another round of nausea.

At night I could hear the many German passengers singing in the lounge over my head. Adam reported that they were raucous and drunk, locking arms and bellowing popular German songs into the early morning hours. We had read enough post-war anti-German literature to hear their songs only in terms of the youth groups and Nazi rallies of the past. Their love of singing together represented to us the worst of the fatherland, and we, along with many other passengers, avoided their nightly gatherings, the newsreels of our childhoods still casting shadows of the German efforts to dominate the western world. By the final two days of the voyage, I could walk the corridors and, on feeling the fresh air on the deck fill my lungs, I learned, almost too late, that the antidote to seasickness was fresh air and keeping my gaze on the horizon.

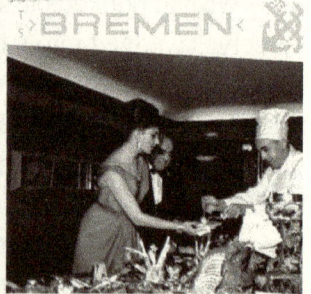

We disembarked at Cherbourg, a small city of 20,000, on Bastille Day. We walked through the heart of the town square, glorying in the sound of the French voices and the smells of the grass and trees. Their fireworks display was modest and brief, the rockets soundlessly exploding above us as French voices joined the small local band to sing "The Marseilles." For me, it was love at first sight.

With our *Europe on $5.00 a Day* in hand, we found a little hotel near the American Embassy, but within days we realized that this hotel was too expensive for us and too far from Adam's old haunts near St. Germain des Pres. Going a rung down the ladder of Frommer-recommended hotels, we moved to a small shabby hotel on Le Rue des Anciennes Comedies. The clerk at L'Hotel de Quatres Nations did not mind seeing us carry a baguette up the four flights of stairs every morning. Almost everyone else in the hotel stashed apples and Camembert in the dresser drawers and made coffee over a small Bunsen burner. Our little room had a bidet, a dresser and a bed. A tiny, usually dirty, toilet and shower were down the hall. Our room's tall, shuttered windows looked out over the cobblestone street teeming with vendors selling newspaper cones of French fries cooked over an open kettle every night. Early every morning, they hawked cheeses, onions, naked hanging chickens and stacks of glass-eyed fish.

On my forays to this market, I learned first-hand that Americans were personae non grata. The prior March, Charles de Gaulle had asked Lyndon Johnson to enter negotiations for the removal of NATO military equipment from France. De Gaulle's disdain for West Germany's dependence on the US and his own desire for France to emerge as a supreme power in Europe fueled anti-Americanism. Gaullist-leaning press railed at the violence, racism, vulgarity, moral laxity and materialism of Americans. Public sentiment against the Americans' escalating involvement in Viet Nam raged; the gratitude of the French for our hand in liberating France in World War II had worn thin. At a Humphrey Bogart film festival, during the newsreel, I saw an American fighter jet shot down over Viet Nam. The film audience cheered riotously. We Americans in the audience were not only foreigners but enemies whose deaths were celebrated.

Our days took on a shape. Adam slept all morning, rising around lunchtime to go with me to the Green Parrot, a cheap little restaurant lined with long communal tables where students, artists and budget tourists gathered. I got up much earlier than Adam and drank an espresso at the café next door. As I began to worry about running out of money, I made coffee over the burner in our room and munched on a piece of baguette spread with Camembert or jam.

Adam had no interest in the museums, venerable churches or traditional tourist sites. He had immediately fallen into the patterns he had when he lived in Paris at age seventeen: drinking coffee, finding an expat to talk with, eating lunch, writing or reading, drinking at a café at night. Adam had no interest in showing Paris to me. If I wanted to go outside the perimeters of his routine, I was on my own. Afternoons, he worked on a short story using Burroughs' cut-up method, and I walked and walked to the Sorbonne, Notre Dame, down the Champs Élysées, into the diplomatic neighborhood, up and down Boulevard St. Germain.

141. PARIS — *Le Panorama des Sept Ponts* C. M.

In 1966, gangs of tourists flocking behind placard-bearing, shrill tour guides had not yet invaded Notre Dame. The French could still go to Mass there in peace, and the priests did not have to compete with the cacophony of the tourist hordes. On a drizzly September afternoon, I walked alone among the massive columns leading to the altar. Pigeons purled and cooed outside the stained-glass windows. I could breathe in the hundreds of years of history, and I could see the medieval architectural features and imagine waves of Gregorian Chant curling upward to the arches above.

Adam chanced upon an old acquaintance from his earlier days in Paris. Daniel Mauroc, a homosexual hanger-on of little talent following early success with *The Evergreen Review*, met us for a drink almost every night. He felt obliged, entitled perhaps, to tell me how wrong my clothes were for me. The harsh chemicals used by neighborhood dry cleaners had ruined the few clothes I had, so when I spent the money to buy a new outfit, Daniel was quick to inform me that the color was terrible, further eroding my confidence.

The only woman I met in the five months we lived in Paris was a Junior Year Abroad student from Brandeis University. She heard my Midwestern accent as she, Adam and I walked down St. Michel Boulevard, and as lifelong New Yorkers sometimes do, she immediately jumped to the conclusion that I was an unschooled redneck. I was the first Midwesterner she had ever met. As we talked about D. H. Lawrence, she directed all her comments to Adam. I resented her easy rejection of me and so made a point of correcting a statement she made about *Women in Love*, my having written a thesis on Lawrence a year earlier. After I challenged her opinion, her pride was injured, and she had no further interest in getting to know either of us; she had just experienced a little cultural dissonance of her own.

The one way I could please Daniel was to cook a traditional American meal for his dinner guests. I fried chicken, mashed potatoes and baked apple pie, As I struggled to produce this hearty farm meal in his tiny Montparnasse apartment, he whispered, "I didn't have money for an appetizer, so I bought this cat food. We'll spread it on bread, and no one will know the difference." To get by as a perpetually struggling artist, he'd grown comfortable and even begun to take delight in deceiving anyone, everyone, friends or enemies. He was right—as the carafes of wine flowed, not a soul suspected they were eating cat food.

We sometimes met Philip Lussier, an expat from Boston, and his lover, Paco, from Spain. Philip, a former public relations executive, stayed in Paris so that he could openly live with Paco, his seventeen-year-old Spanish lover, and drink as much as he needed to. Philip seemed to be living on a trust fund or inheritance; Paco kept their studio apartment clean and sometimes worked as a waiter. It was Paco who introduced me to the one-burner cooking idea when he taught me to make Crepes Suzette.

One night when the four of us walked down Boulevard St. Michel on our way back to our neighborhood, Philip was very drunk and staggered down the street, his brown eyes bleary. On this hot summer night, police swarmed through the university area trying to prevent rioting students from barricading streets. Philip screamed at drivers of cars trying to wend their way through the blocked, congested streets. He charged a stalled car, raising his scrawny leg waist high to kick the door of the car. Taking Philip by the elbows, we turned into an alleyway until the car had gone, then crept through back streets to get back to our hotels. Paco helped Philip up the three floors to their apartment, once more steering his middle-aged lover away from screaming obscenities in French Canadian at passersby.

The writers we met were not destined to become our generation's Ernest Hemingway, Henry Miller or Allen Ginsburg. Though I once saw James Baldwin hanging out at Les Deux Magots, the writers we knew were probably going nowhere. They had come to Paris to live out a fantasy and often to hide, drink or feed an addiction. I suspected that Adam and I, his dreamy, naïve wife, were no different. Adam's stories never seemed to get finished, and when I told him that we were going to run out of money, he did not seem to be able to take in the information. He was not looking for a job, and I came to know that he had no intention of finding work. I was coming to understand that the man I had thought knowledgeable about managing to live abroad had no practical survival skills at all. He was stuck in his earlier Paris life funded by his grandmother's money and had never held a job. If we were going to avoid the disaster I saw coming, I was going to have to find the way to do it.

I began to try to find ways to save money. Using the small Bantam paperback I'd purchased, *The Art of French Cooking*, I looked for recipes we could both afford and cook over our Bunsen burner. I remembered that in the US, the cheapest meats of all were the organ meats, liver and kidney. The recipe for Kidneys Madeira seemed possible, though neither of us had ever eaten kidney.

Veal Kidney with Port Wine

4 veal kidneys
¼ tsp freshly ground pepper
¼ cup flour
pinch of nutmeg
2 tablespoons butter
1 tablespoon chopped parsley
2 tablespoons port wine
½ teaspoon salt
6 slices French bread, fried in butter

Remove outer skin from kidneys and cut them into slices ½ in thick. Dredge with flour. In a large, heavy skillet, heat butter. Add kidneys and cook over brisk flame, turning them often, for 10 minutes, or until browned on all sides. Do not overcook. Remove meat to heated serving dish and keep warm. To pan, add port wine, salt, pepper and nutmeg and heat until the brown parts which stick to the bottom of the pan are dissolved. Do not allow to boil. Pour over meat. Sprinkle with parsley. Garnish with fried bread. Serve hot.

When I asked for kidney at the newly opened supermarket, the butcher was incredulous. "You want *four kidneys*?" he asked.

"Oui, monsieur," I answered confidently.

"Come back on Wednesday afternoon," he said.

The day I picked up the kidneys, he handed them to me to take to the checkout line, still shaking his head unbelievingly. "It will be 16 francs," he said.

Finally, I understood. The cost of the kidneys surpassed the cost of six nights' lodgings at our hotel. I had just custom-ordered, without knowing it, a delicacy. The bloody package was now in my hands. I couldn't return it, and I couldn't pay for it. I walked around and around the aisles of the supermarket, thinking about abandoning the package on a shelf and running away. If I got caught shoplifting, I would possibly be jailed and, if I was lucky, deported rather than left in prison. Sweating, I slipped out of the store with the package surrounded by a throng of French office workers picking up dinner ingredients before they headed home. Having a good education and a sturdy moral upbringing could and would collapse under conditions of fear and desperation.

My uninvited education into myself, my deepening awareness of Adam's inability to live on his own and my cultural naiveté eroded my sense of worth and safety and diminished the delight I took in the City of Light. By September, I was hired to teach a conversation class for Massey-Ferguson executives at their plant in the suburbs, and I was pregnant. Lurching back into Paris on the rush-hour subway after class made me deathly ill. My stress level escalated when I thought of our expired visas, our dwindling savings, and my lack of prenatal care. The police had stepped up their efforts to clear homeless Beatniks from beneath the bridges where they slept at night. Rumors of police brutality and their antipathy toward indigent Americans swept through the expat community on the Left Bank. When I began to bleed, I knew I was in danger of a miscarriage. We went to a hospital in the suburbs, and I was given the preventive injection blamed years later for malformed uteruses and the resultant infertility in the surviving offspring. I did not know the danger posed by the injection, but even if I had known, I probably had no choice if I wanted to bring my baby to term.

As I faced the reality of our situation, I stepped up my effort to get a job teaching for the University of Maryland in Europe. We would have to leave Paris, but the visa issue would be resolved, and I would be able to get medical care. In November, when the offer to teach an eight-week course in freshman composition in Germany came through, I grabbed it.

Adam and I were housed in the Bachelor Officers' Quarters at Kassel-Rothwesten Airfield. The only other person in the barracks was a lieutenant we never saw. We occasionally heard his ghostly steps echoing in the empty corridor outside our little twin-bedded room when he returned from a night out. The army base was tucked into a heavily wooded small mountainside near Kassel, West Germany.

The officers' quarters and surrounding buildings had been built by the Luftwaffe in 1935 and taken over by the U. S. Army in 1945. In the Enlisted Men's Cafeteria where we ate, the walls behind us still eerily retained the murals painted there during the time it was used as a Bierkeller by German airmen and, in 1944, Russian prisoners of war. Little brown-shirted warriors with machine guns scurried across the brown and beige murals to their aircraft; bombs and broken, wounded American planes dove to the ground. Germans had used the base to train the German soldiers to kill and now, sitting beneath the murals of the hated Nazi were young American men my age filing past with their cafeteria trays; in a few short weeks, they would be pounding North Vietnamese villages, women and children.

During my interview with the base commander, I was informed that Adam and I would be unable to ride the bus, which regularly followed a route from the base to the city of Kassel.

"You can't go on the bus," the commander said. "It would be too dangerous. When the men go off base, they get drunk and out of control. You wouldn't be safe." The commander's receptionist, a German citizen, later told me that these men were brutalizing the citizenry, tearing up old men's candy stalls at train stations, brawling, breaking store windows and trampling flowers in public gardens. When city officials complained to the commander, he clenched his fist, pounding it on the desk.

"I want them this way. I feed them raw hamburger!" he said. "We're getting them ready for war."

We were confined to the base for the eight weeks we were there. Hiring a cab was financially prohibitive, and, as the commander said, we didn't dare brave riding with our revved-up, rabid countrymen. The one other resident in our building had a car, but we never had a chance to make his acquaintance. One weekend shortly after we arrived, we heard no footsteps in the corridor on Saturday night. On Monday morning, the commander's receptionist told me that he had smashed his car into a tree as he drove the winding mountain road back toward the base and had died. Adam wrote in our room in those weeks, sitting rocking on the edge of the bed and staring owl-like at the walls from behind his huge plastic-rimmed glasses.

I found the base library and spent the days there, preparing lesson plans and reading whatever I could find. I studied the rhetoric of the Army newspaper, *Stars and Stripes*, simultaneously fascinated and appalled. The formula for the front page was to report on recent battles in Viet Nam, using language laced with violent verbs such as "butchered" and "smashed." The nouns used to refer to the North Vietnamese soldiers were inevitably dehumanizing: "gooks" and "Commies." In a column adjacent to these reports of devastating war triumphs were human interest stories featuring sentimental stories of home and holiday or a sweet furry puppy drinking beer through a straw from a wholesome-looking All-American soldier.

I enjoyed preparing for my weekly class; I certainly had plenty of time to thoroughly prepare for it. The young men in my class were graduates of the Monterey Language Institute and, as a group, were the best freshman composition students I ever had. At Rothwesten, they were "ditty-boppers," soldiers assigned to intercept and translate radio transmissions from East Germany only a few miles away. They stared at my growing belly, and finally, one stayed after class to delicately ask if I was pregnant and went on to quietly confirm that there were indeed subjects that they could neither write nor talk about. The students and I learned to do a little dance. If I ever got too close to some topic they had been told was "off-limits," they smiled and looked indulgently down at their books. I veered away from the topic, and our discussion resumed.

Most of my time in the library was now spent poring over the Sears catalog and compiling a list of what Dr. Spock had decreed mothers needed for their layette. Toward the end of the eight weeks, I saw an Army doctor. I told him that my next assignment for the University of Maryland was to be in Ankara, Turkey.

"No," he said. "You can't go there. You would be at high risk of getting amoebic dysentery and losing the baby. Get another plan."

"What other plan?" I thought. "There isn't one."

I decided to telegram my parents and ask for the money to fly home, a humiliating admission of my foolhardiness. Getting the money to fly back to the States came as a *deus ex machina* solution. Money suddenly dropped from the sky in the form of an airmail letter. As I was gearing up to send the telegram to my parents, a letter came from Leona containing a check for a thousand dollars. She had sent the money to Adam for Christmas and envisioned that we would use it to have a Merry Christmas for ourselves—buy some Italian wallets, French perfume or cashmere sweaters. Within hours, the check was cashed, and I had booked our tickets to fly home.

Icelandic Air was the first "budget travel" airline and the darling of artists and students flying between Europe and North America. As soon as the course ended, we were on Icelandic Air, bound first for a stopover in Reykjavík for re-fueling and then for New York City. We landed in Reykjavík in a white-out snowstorm. As I looked out the plane window, ambulances and fire trucks edged the runway, and I realized that the pilot had just made a scary blind landing. We had to take a cab into Reykjavik to wait until the grounded turbo-prop plane could safely take off for New York City, where the same snowstorm awaited.

One of the worst snowstorms of the century shrouded New York City. The plane circled the airport again and again, unable to get clearance to land on the snow-choked airstrip. My re-entry into America was ironic: as the plane glided over the Statue of Liberty, I could not keep back the nausea from the endless circling, and I violently threw up in the paper airbag, hearing the collective groan of beleaguered fellow passengers as we descended. In the airport, strident patriotic band music, flags and uniforms were everywhere: soldiers, sailors, armed guards. In our absence, the number of American military people in Viet Nam had soared from 190,000 in January 1966 to 389,000 in 1967. When the New Year's bells rang in 1967, 6,000 American troops had been killed in 1966 and 30,000 wounded that same year.

Within days, the Iron Triangle Offensive would begin. My oldest nephew was one of the lucky wounded. In the first month of his tour of duty, he was wounded in Viet Nam and sent home, his thigh bone shattered, but not beyond repair. I did not know, until almost fifty years later, that another nephew, haunted by what his government ordered him to do with his excellent marksmanship at age eighteen, would take his own life. The battle over Viet Nam in America was an intimate war, family member against family member locked in an angry, anguished embrace.

The disillusionment and chaos in my life continued against this backdrop of discord and aggression. The snowstorm brought New York to a standstill: most stores closed, streets silent and blocked with snow, planes, trains and buses resting in place. One of Adam's old girlfriends lived in Manhattan, and Adam called her to ask if we could stay with her while we waited to get back to my parents' farm. She had no space but called a friend of hers to get us a place for the night. We found ourselves bedded down with a psychotic. As I lay exhausted in a sheet blackened with soil, he muttered wildly over the long Japanese bayonets he sharpened on the other side of the dim studio apartment. I watched him pace and parry with his blades, wondering when he would turn on us. When he finally fell asleep, we slipped the multiple bolts on the door and plunged into the cold dawn, leaving our luggage behind in order not to awaken him.

I was able to reach a college friend studying at the Manhattan School of Music, and she took us in. Her familiar Northern Missouri accent and the tiny gray kitten she had just adopted from the Humane

Society calmed me. Within hours, the kitten began to sicken, and with the city still paralyzed by snow, there was no vet clinic open or accessible. Distemper had already been incubating in her at the Humane Society, and she died convulsing in my hands. The death of the kitten hit me hard. I had nurtured and played with cats since childhood, so the kitten was emblematic of affectionate normalcy rooted deep within me.

When we got to Missouri, I had a few days to rest at home before I saw that my parents weren't going to be able to tolerate my husband's nocturnal wandering and his inability to handle any responsibility. With enough money to last three or four months, we moved to an apartment in Lawrence to wait for the birth of our baby in May. I would be using that time to line up a teaching job for fall. I now fully understood that the safety and security of my baby and me were perched squarely on my swollen lap.

Postcards from the Southwest

Two wondrous events took place in 1967: the birth of my daughter and my introduction to the Southwest. As I waddled heavily down the sunbaked brick streets of Lawrence, I could only think of getting the birthing on its way. Amy was two or more weeks late, and I felt miserable in the unseasonably hot weather of late May. Maybe this long walk back home from the doctor's office would start my labor.

The doctor had told me that if my water broke, I should go to the hospital right away. If not, I should wait until the labor contractions were five minutes apart and then check in. My water broke at around 9:30 pm, and so we made the trip to the hospital. The nurses who first examined me were crisp and curt, not at all happy to see me.

"What are you doing here?" one snapped at me. "You aren't even in labor."

"My water broke, and the doctor told me to come in if that happened," I answered, surprised at the nurse's sharp, critical tone.

With a disbelieving snort, she grudgingly began to prepare me for the labor room. My being there "so soon" was clearly a violation of protocol in her view. The crabby nurse informed us that Adam was going to be permitted to visit me in the labor room but would be banned from the delivery room. After several hours of the labor process slowly ramping up, Adam was sent home to get some sleep. I lay in the labor room for hours with nurses coming and going at long intervals, each time making me feel guilty for being there or asking for anything. The nurses' lack of communication and scolding attitude walled me into the shot-induced "twilight sleep," a semi-dozing, sometimes sharply painful isolation. The point of the amnesic drug I had been given was to cause the mother to forget undergoing the birthing process rather than to blunt pain.

For me, the shot wasn't strong enough. I still remember the pain and loneliness I experienced in that room. By mid-afternoon the next day, the nurses deemed it appropriate to call the doctor and Adam to the hospital, the doctor for the delivery, and Adam to appear after the deed was done. I was a slab of meat strapped to a gurney for my "safety," I was told—not a person who felt pain, confusion and abandonment. Only six years later, when I read *Our Bodies, Ourselves*, did I understand that I was not singled out for this lonely misery because I was somehow discovered to be a radical or unpatriotic misfit. I was one of thousands of women going through the standard birthing process of the mid-1960s.

When I woke from the fog, Amy was lying across my stomach. She was beautiful and alert from the beginning, already reaching with her arms to embrace the world and to catch my heart forever. She even looked like the little girl I envisioned on those solitary afternoons when I paged through the Sears Catalog in the library at Rothwesten; I had somehow known that the baby would be a girl and that she would look like this.

For the week I was in the hospital, the nurses and I continued to clash. I had read in the baby books about "rooming in," and had asked for that prior to Amy's birth. By having the baby in a bed next to mine during the first days of life, the mother and baby would bond to each other earlier, and the transition back home would be smoother. The nurses wanted none of this radical idea!

"It's not a good idea! It isn't sanitary, and you won't get your rest. What if something goes wrong?"

Having agreed earlier to let me try the "rooming-in" idea, the doctor over-ruled Nurse Mary, and she did not take that well. When Adam later visited Amy and me in the room, Nurse Mary swooped into the room, her beak-like nose and jaw jutting forward.

"Get off that bed. Visitors are not allowed to sit on the edge of the patient's bed."

When I left the hospital, there were no fond farewells or good wishes, rather eye-rolling at these wayward parents with their far-out ideas. The draconian rules and rigid clinical attitudes of hospital staff at that time were about to change with the emergence of the Lamaze method two years later, and it was not going to be a change those nurses liked.

As soon as I was able to walk to campus, I went to the English as a Second Language Department office to see if any jobs had been posted. My boss saw me there.

"Do you want to go to Colorado? Could you be there in two weeks?"

By the third week in June, Adam, three-week-old Amy, and I began the drive to Durango, the turquoise and white '57 Chevy packed with our few possessions. Adam had never learned to drive, so I headed across the wheat fields of Kansas to climb toward Wolf Creek Pass and snake around the hairpin curves.

My new job was to teach English in a Title III program meant to help Native American students from across the continent succeed in their coursework and stay in college. The program was housed at Fort Lewis College, a four-year college admitting students tuition-free if their ethnic origins were at least 25 percent Native American. The honor students at their respective schools, the freshman came from their first nation homes in Alaska, South Dakota, New Mexico, Arizona, Colorado and Montana. Hanging over their heads was a college dropout rate for Native Americans of 90 percent. Cultural differences and poor academic preparation presented nearly insurmountable barriers for them. At home, many of their parents lived in shacks, dilapidated mobile homes, cars and hogans. Poverty, alcoholism and disease shredded their families and traditional cultures.

The Title III staff of four (a director, an academic counselor and two English as a Second Language instructors) threw itself into getting the program moving. Only one of us, the director, had direct experience in working with Native American populations, but we all plunged into the building of the program, building the bicycle as we rode it. Our counselor did what he had always done with a new group of freshmen—gave them a battery of tests. In 1967, it wasn't yet broadly understood that standard IQ tests were culture-bound and had little or no validity in measuring the intelligence of non-white, culturally diverse students. These honors students, the brightest of their nations, registered scores putting them into the IQ ranges lower than average intelligence! We were crest-fallen and humbled as we took in the implications of our first big mistake. The results vanished with no reports given to the students.

Day after day, students in my class sat quietly looking down at their desks, passively resisting my questions. I had immersed myself in reading about their cultures, learning that, in their worlds, looking me in the eye was offensive. How could I teach them to ask questions, venture answers or discuss concepts? They were diffident about their homework, fearing failure and not seeing the urgency of doing the work at a particular time, their views of time and timeliness vastly different from those of us "Anglos." If exploring concepts in class and skill-building through the practice represented by homework were not going to work, what could happen in the class? The students were not enjoying this exercise in treading water, and neither was I, but how could we change the situation?

On weekends, local sons and daughters of the area, faculty and staff vacated the campus, leaving the two small dorms in the hands of young resident assistants. Our program students were the only other people in the dorms on weekends. Most were unable to visit their families and villages, so they relied only on each other for support and social activities. Adam and I invited the students to come to supper on a Sunday night and spent days and a major part of our grocery money preparing vats of spaghetti and salad. On the night of the gathering, we sat alone in our house and waited for guests to arrive who would never show up. As she helped me learn to make fry bread, Gloria Medicinehorse from South Dakota told me that it was more thoughtful in her culture to not show up rather than to directly say "no" to an invitation. I was learning, mostly through failure, how wide the gap was between our cultures.

People who taught these students had to learn to accept that most of their students were going to fail and to absorb that information without falling into despair or indifference. Any one student who succeeded was a major victory. I watched as a Navajo student, Barney Mitchell, stopped attending classes and returned to his Arizona home for longer and longer periods. He had recently published a nationally recognized novel, but the lack of support of his zealous (perhaps over-zealous) editor/teacher in Arizona, his loneliness and fear of failure, and his drinking put an end to his college career. He could not maintain his image as an independently talented writer and preferred to withdraw.

One of our brightest, most promising students, Marjorie, appeared puffy-faced in my office on a Monday morning.

"I am leaving school," she said, "and going back to my Aleutian village."

"Why?" I asked, seeing she had been crying.

"Because I am pregnant. I am being kicked out of college tomorrow."

When I told the program director, a career superintendent of Bureau of Indian Affairs schools, his face reddened angrily. He strode across campus to the administration offices to beg for an exception to the rules for our top student. He could not overcome the administrators' resistance to allowing her to continue, and so we watched her drive away to catch a plane in Denver with neither her Apache boyfriend nor a completed year of college.

To understand our students better, we traveled to the students' homelands—Shiprock for the Navajo, Canyon de Chelly where the ancient cliff-dwellers had lived, Taos Pueblo. When we stood outside Taos Pueblo on a December night to watch the Deer Dance, I sensed the timelessness of the generations and the deep spiritual devotion of the people who had performed this ceremony across the ages. I had felt this same way when I first saw Notre Dame in Paris. Ghostly figures wrapped in white blankets move silently and quickly in and out of pueblo doors and vanished down narrow interior passageways. Finally, the dancers emerged, dancing slowly and ritualistically around a circle, their deerskin breeches, and deer antler headdresses in low contrast beneath the cold moon-lit sky. As we had been instructed to do, we Anglo onlookers watched silently from a distance and, just as quietly, went back to our cars after the dancers vanished back into the pueblo. The dance, this spiritual connection to their people, was part of what some students were unwilling to trade for a life and livelihood outside the reservation.

On a sleepy, frustrating spring afternoon, I made a minor break-through in my Introduction to Literature class. As usual, the students had not read the play and passively waited for me to give up on asking questions. Instead, I assigned them parts to read aloud. The class atmosphere changed totally—students leaned forward, intently listening to each other and visibly reacting to the sad desperation of Willie Loman as they made their way through the script of *Death of a Salesman*. Of course! They came from an oral tradition—hearing the language, their empathy for a person trapped in a world he could not understand or function in grabbed their spirits. If I wanted to reach them in class, I would have to start from their own way of examining the human condition and move from there. I was increasingly drawn to learn about the history and culture of Native Americans and to grapple with educational strategies for reaching them.

At home, my marriage, held together by the barest of flimsy threads, continued to unravel. The first place we had rented in the summer was a log cabin tucked into the birches and pines off a steep mountain road. During the summer and early autumn months, we savored the scent of the pines, the music of the swaying birch leaves above our heads, and the turning of the birches to a mass of gold leaves.

One weekend we took our tent and set up camp further up the mountain. As we sat near the campfire on Saturday night, we heard a car radio blasting music through the windows of a car coming our way. Loud male voices bellowed above the music. As the car careened along the mountain road, the men must have seen our campfire in the woods. A gunshot whistled over our heads. I dropped to a prone position, holding five-month-old Amy to my chest as I crawled behind our parked car. We waited, listening in the darkness, for the car to return or for other gunshots. Moments later, as the silence continued, we hastily jumped into the car and drove back to our cabin, leaving our tent and gear behind until the next day. When I told a local resident what had happened, he said, "Oh yeah—Texans. They come up here during hunting season and get roaring drunk. They shoot at other hunters, through café windows, and at our cattle, thinking they've spotted a moose. We all go into hiding when they come."

I didn't feel safe anywhere. On most days, Adam stayed at the cabin alone, supposedly writing a book of short stories. The teachers at Fort Lewis College were largely unaware of the Title III staff. They did not cross paths with us as we worked in our offices at the edge of the campus. For most, their social lives revolved around their acreages in the country and their horses.

We met only one couple during the year, and Adam managed to alienate them within two weeks. Mark Grove, the new professor, his wife, Adam, and I went to dinner, joyfully sharing our common philosophies and political views. Mark and Adam talked writers and writing all evening, savoring the prospect of finding a kindred spirit in the arid Anamosa Valley. A couple of weeks after Mark and Adam exchanged drafts of their short stories, Mark glowered at me whenever we met on the campus sidewalk and strode angrily past. I was stunned by the abrupt change and stung when our invitations to meet up with them were curtly declined.

I cornered Mark in his office on a Monday morning.

"What's going on?" I demanded.

He wouldn't answer.

"I don't understand."

"Don't you?"

"No," I said.

"Adam has stolen my work and inserted it into his own story," Mark said icily.

"What?"

"Yes! Took it for his own. We don't want to see you anymore." His cold dismissive stare backed me out his office door.

In my office, I faced for the first time that Adam could not tell the difference between the reality he encountered on the page and the reality of his own life. He believed that Mark's words were his. Did anything he told me about his life in Paris with William Burroughs and Allen Ginsburg actually happen? Adam had indeed spent his late teen years in Paris, but was any of the rest of it true? Had he merged, without knowing it, his own fragile identity with events in Burroughs' life?

I remembered that Burroughs killed his wife during a drunken episode, and, for the first time, I was scared. I did not know a name for what I had just identified, but I knew something more serious than I had ever let myself see walked with Adam in my own house. It was beyond a writer's passion to live the writer's life, beyond the bohemian lifestyle, beyond refusing to grow up. I had to find a way to live with the insanity, to protect myself and Amy. My over-ripe innocence fell to the ground at the same time America's love affair with itself came crashing down.

Adam spent more and more hours of the day doing nothing but rocking on the edge of the bed and playing scenes from his current story over and over in his head. His days and nights were reversed. He listened to *Sergeant Pepper's Lonely Hearts Club Band* hour after hour through the night, finally falling asleep at five in the morning and sleeping until afternoon. Realizing that I could not trust him to take care of Amy, I took her into Durango each morning to stay with Mrs. Aspromante, a wonderfully gentle babysitter. I never knew what to expect when I returned to the cabin at the end of the day. Adam stacked the dirty dishes for days, each day promising to complete the only responsibility he had. On one afternoon, I entered the cabin to discover that he had smashed every dish we owned against the wall and had no memory of doing it. His condition, beyond my experience or understanding, was deteriorating.

By late fall, the snow-packed mountain roads were already too much for my nerves. I had to stay alive for Amy. A snowstorm blasted the area at Christmas. We had started to drive to Missouri but found out in Durango that Wolf Creek Pass was closed. By that time, the snow was falling so fast and hard that we couldn't go back to the cabin either. We spent the holiday in a cheap motel in Durango, looking out on the frozen, empty streets. I could not be sure that I would be able to make it to class as the winter weather worsened. We moved to an empty ranch house near town and, on some Saturday nights, drove into Durango for dinner and drinks at the Diamond Belle, a beautifully preserved bar from the wild boomtown days of silver mining in the mountains nearby.

On these nights out, Adam drank heavily, unwilling to come out of his alcohol daze and leave the bar where on those off-season nights, we were the only patrons listening to the honky-tonk, ragtime piano player.

As he ordered his fourth cocktail, I searched for a way out of the misery. A move to Albuquerque seemed to be a way for me to right myself. I could pursue my interest in bi-cultural, bilingual studies, and, I hoped, Adam could move forward in some way. Because he had not attended high school beyond the age of seventeen, he had completed his GED at Menninger's Clinic. He was a smart man who loved reading. Could he get a college education? Would that give his life some new purpose? I applied for and was granted admission to the new Linguistics and Language Pedagogy program at the University of New Mexico and a teaching fellowship.

The five years that followed my graduation from college had turned upside down everything I had thought I had known about the way the world worked. I felt dispirited and very, very tired—tired of chaos, tired of disappointment, tired of a life without affection or friendship, tired of having to carry the whole load. The move to Albuquerque was a desperate, probably doomed, effort to achieve stability.

On the morning of our move, Adam drove the eight miles into Durango to get the U-Haul trailer we would use to take our belongings to Albuquerque while I stayed at the house to pack. The sun climbed to its noon position and beyond. By mid-afternoon, Adam still had not returned. I figured out that he had probably gone to his favorite restaurant and bar for lunch, so I called there. The bartender told me that Adam was there, well into a lavish meal and a bottle of wine. The money for the U-Haul was enough to cover the restaurant tab.

As Amy crawled among the tunnels of packed boxes and peered, smiling at me, around the sides of our loaded suitcases, I stared out the window toward the road. By the time Adam careened up the gravel road, we only had time to return to Durango before the U-Haul company closed and pay for the trailer with our little remaining cash. We slept among the boxes that night on our bare mattress and the next morning loaded the trailer and began our descent into the high desert country where Albuquerque, another point of reckoning, waited.

Rose Ann Findlen

The Center Cannot Hold

We drove down the mountains and into the valley, snaking through seedy, sprawling Albuquerque by way of Central Avenue, more famously known as Route 66. Squat dusty motels and tired restaurants with cracked vinyl booths lined the avenue on either side. Our sway-backed old white Buick spewed black smoke from its behind, dusting the sides of the U-Haul we towed, our belongings jostling and banging together behind us.

I had brought us to Albuquerque not so much to embrace a new life as to run from a string of lonely mismatches with people and places: Normal, Illinois, Paris, Rothwesten, and Durango. Adam and I had lived in four places since our marriage, and each time we had to move. In Normal and Durango, Adam stood out like a bizarre crow in his limp wool overcoat, his offbeat language and permanently enlarged left pupil signaling "drugs," "crazy," "erratic, weird acts." We could never fit in or be accepted in those communities and, to be fair, did not want to. Certainly, there was no place for us on a Viet Nam-era Army base, and, in Paris, we would have starved.

I increasingly understood that I could never be happy with—or possibly even safe with—the father of my child. I drove into Albuquerque hoping to find a place big enough to have a community, academic or artistic, where Adam could somehow fit in. I had always managed to find a way to succeed in school, so it was to the university that I went to look for belonging and a possible future. After four moves and three friendless years, I needed people who might understand me and, even, care about me.

If the ancient sea, now turned desert, had been full of water, our Buick would have been a boat rocking rudderless, "in chains." In the summer of 1968, I was adrift, the electric charges shooting through America knocking me and the country from one magnetic field to another. I am told that ocean-going vessels need gyrocompasses to find True North. The standard magnetic compasses cannot withstand the pull of ferrous metals or electric current. My internal compass, all I had to rely on, could only spin amid the electrical charges and tell me I was lost.

I had made the decision to leave Durango months earlier as Adam, Amy and I sat in a hotel lounge in Durango on Christmas Day, unable to go over Wolf Creek Pass to spend the holidays with our families. We were without friends or family, Adam could never stop at just one, or even two cocktails, and I could not see a future for us in the conservative ranch community that had not yet become an upscale tourist destination.

Amy was nineteen months old in January 1968, a year that historians later called "defining" for our country. As I juggled the challenges of living with Adam, motherhood, and a teaching job that, by definition, involved coming to terms with sad failure after sad failure, I began to understand that I would have to plan for my future in a much more deliberate, realistic way than I had ever done before. I had been raised with the notion that if I married someone, I married that someone forever, no matter what. As a mother, I now had a little girl whose life depended on me; she needed stability. As a teacher, I realized that little I had been taught or had experienced in the classroom contributed to helping my Native American students succeed in college. I needed to know more. My life direction had reached an intersection with no recognizable landmarks.

I made the decision on my own, but Adam happily went along because he hated Durango. Adam never thought about planning or even the future. He lived from day to day, from meal to meal, from drink to drink, and, at the end of every month, panicked because, without fail, he had run out of money. Cursing his millionaire grandmother for her stinginess, each month, he called his trust officer to find out when his monthly allotment would arrive. When we were dating, I had believed that he had chosen to live on his meager allowance so that he could spend his days writing. The story fit my romantic notion of the starving poet. I had not yet seen that he would never be able to hold a job because of the mental illness that held him in its grip.

In Durango, what we knew of world and national events came to us through the nightly news on television. Our social isolation and the culture of the ranching and mining western town made us feel as if we were on a different planet watching the goings-on of Earth. We had watched in disbelief the replays of footage on the balcony where Martin Luther King was shot. We saw the crowds thronging around Bobby Kennedy's mortally wounded body. We heard reports of grossly inflated counts of Viet Cong casualties and saw the photo of a South Viet Nam officer murdering a captured Viet Cong soldier following the first day of the Tet Offensive.

While Amy ate her applesauce and wound up her bright red Fisher-Price musical clock one more time, we saw a Vietnamese girl, naked and burned, running from their napalmed villages in Eddie Morgan's stark black and white image. The American image of itself as God's gift to the world, a country of compassionate, noble guardians of the democratic ideals, crashed and burned along with those distant villages. Our cultural landmarks emerged as unreliable identifiers of our national character.

Throughout the spring and summer of 1968, we had stood before the television in our little ranch house outside Durango watching the peace movement become violent, the Civil Rights movement lose Martin Luther King to an assassin, followed two months later by the murder of the prince of Camelot, Robert Kennedy, in the back kitchen of a hotel. Richard Nixon, the prince of darkness, and his super-bigot Spiro Agnew, spewing invectives against "effete intellectuals," were in their ascendancy.

In Durango that year, the biggest news had to do with the drunken Texan shooting through diner windows in hunting season, the opening of a laundromat or the improvements on the Silverton narrow gauge railroad. There were no African Americans, no hippies, not even any liberals to disturb the peace.

Albuquerque and the University of New Mexico became our new destination that spring. Maybe there, I could get a doctor's degree and a tenure-track job. Maybe there would be kindred spirits for us. Maybe there would be professors who could teach me how to reach the Native American students, and maybe there would be others who abhorred the war and the racism tearing at our country's soul.

We drove onto Dartmouth Avenue to the little post-war adobe house near the university, hoping to find a future. My graduate assistant salary and Adam's allotment were not going to be enough to meet our expenses, so I encouraged Adam to get a part-time job. A drugstore chain hired him to pick up exposed camera film each morning and return developed pictures to the various drugstore locations in the valley. Within days Adam gleefully reported how he stopped off at local bars for drinks and then made up for the lost time by careening at 70 miles an hour through Bernalillo and the suburbs of Albuquerque. In a delivery run when he was especially late, he locked himself out of the car late at night in a crime-ridden neighborhood in central Albuquerque. I somehow got to the location and jimmied open the car window, constantly looking over my shoulder into the dark as Adam stood holding Amy at the edge of the street. He happily took my suggestion that he quit the job and, once again, I was reminded that he probably could not ever hold any job. Everything was going to be up to me, counter to the concept of married life presented in the *Ladies' Journal* magazines of my youth or through observation of my parents' sturdy farm partnership.

I ran back into the arms of academe. My graduate advisor was a luminary freshly recruited from the University of Indiana to establish an interdisciplinary program combining linguistics, education and anthropology. As newcomers to the University of New Mexico, we both found ourselves creating our respective plans as we went. Two of the classes we chose were anthropology courses—subjects I had never studied. The anthropology professor was another newcomer to UNM from MIT. He was full of himself and his new elevated rank. When I asked to enroll as a graduate student in his American Indian course, I immediately recognized from his smug, arrogant tone and the way he looked at me that he disdained the intellect of women or of people enrolled in education courses. He agreed to let me enroll when he heard my advisor's name, but he had already decided I was a loser.

Students thronged to his classes. He was new to the university and young. Anthropology was an enticing major for students living amid centuries of Pueblo and Navajo culture, attending annual corn festivals, and seeing the artisans squatting on blankets, their turquoise and pottery arrayed, in Old Town. In 1968, there were no networked computers to keep track of the enrollments taking place in departments throughout the campus, so professors had no idea how many students would appear for a given class on the first day. Professor Bruce's "Introduction to Anthropology: The American Indian" class was jammed with students seated and lining the walls of the room. He needed to cut the size of the class by a third. He pulled out the first-day-of-class chestnut.

Staring at us sternly he said, "Look to your right and to your left. By the end of this course two of you will not be here."

Right.

I was already digging into my familiar reaction to male authority figures setting obstacles in my path. The voices of my derisive brothers teasing me in childhood rang in my ears.

I will be here, you son of a bitch.

At midterm, Dr. Bruce required the graduate students in the class to submit topics for a hefty term paper assignment. When I told him I wanted to examine the function of the peyote cult in the Pan-American Indian culture, he rolled his eyes and sneered. Immediately he assumed that I was a dewy-eyed hippie wanting to elevate the place of peyote (and presumably other drugs) among some tribal groups and, by extension, in our own society. He grudgingly agreed that I could research the topic but was looking forward to handing me "a graduate C." His first response to me throughout the course had always been to approach me as a dim-witted female major in education.

I marched defiantly to the library, fuming at his smirking side glances at the male graduate assistants in the course. How sweet it was on the day he returned the paper marked with an "A."

"This is a fine theoretical paper," he said, his voice revealing his surprise. I could tell by looking at the check-out card in the references I'd used that he had sent his graduate assistants to see whether I had plagiarized. Rosie: 1; Dr. Bruce: 0.

Just as they had been in my master's program at KU, all my professors in my current program were male. While most of my professors were not as overtly hostile to women as Dr. Bruce, their preference for the male graduate students was evident. I had no time to hang out in the departmental office, and so, the professors got to know my male counterparts. In addition, the professors were not sure how to relate to women graduate students as potential colleagues: we were considered more as brainy high school teachers than as university professors. They were envisioning departments full of male professors, just as theirs was, and secondary teachers, who were predominantly female, taking courses from them.

"Hey, Warren," I heard a professor say to a classmate, "come to my office. I want to show you a job opening that I just heard of."

Warren and I were at the same point in our program, and our grades were nearly identical, but to me, he said, "How is your daughter doing?"

Across the country, women engaging in civil rights and war protests were growing weary of smiling sweetly at the testosterone-pumped male leaders and fetching them coffee and sandwiches. I had seen them sitting cross-legged at their lovers' feet at KU as the virile young men, feeling exhilaratingly potent and alive, planned the next day's sit-in. Members of the New York chapter of the National Organization of Women and others gathered to burn their bras in "ashcans of freedom" at the Miss America pageant. For the first time, administrators at Yale were meeting to consider enrolling women. The rising tide of the Second Wave of Feminism gave voice to the feminism that first began for me when I burned with hurt and anger at my brothers' taunts. I chafed at the unfairness of how free they felt to put down my affectionate overtures or the joy I took in my little girl accomplishments. My experience of a male-dominated university environment and my reading of feminist writing at the University of Kansas solidified my anger at male authority figures and male-dominated institutions trying to dictate my place in the world. I faced the world economically, professionally and emotionally on my own. I had little patience left for men standing in my way.

Rod, a clear-eyed, focused graduate of Brigham Young University, symbolized the entitled position of the male doctoral student. He and I were benign competitors in the program. Rod (an appropriate name, I thought) was a rigid, intensely ambitious man with a wife "putting hubby through" by working as a nurse at night and taking care of their two small children by day. He always arrived in class having read all the supplemental material the professor had mentioned during the previous class. I felt that it was a good day if I had read the textbook assignment. I knew I needed to do better than that. I wondered why the books recommended as foundational reading in our linguistics class were always missing from the shelf when I went to find them in the library. One day I followed Rod out of the classroom and trailed behind him as he bolted for the library. Aha! He was scooping up the books immediately after each class! A few hours after following his crewcut hair and sharply pressed Khaki pants moving briskly toward the library, I strolled around the perimeters of the stacks to find his carrel. Yes, secured there for the semester were the all-important readings for the course. I knew when he wouldn't be in his carrel from some prior conversations about his schedule, so I let him scoop up the books after class each day and then read them whenever I could in his sacred space.

One thing Rod and I did have in common was that we were both married with children. At KU, I had a single woman's freedom to explore ideas and develop social relationships. Here, unlike Rod, I had no wife to take care of matters at home. Certainly, my relationship with Adam was more that of caregiver than partner. Nothing in Adam's sad upbringing prepared him to live as an independent adult, let alone as a husband or father. Unlike Rod, I couldn't spend hours sequestered in a study carrel. I had to squeeze my reading and writing into days already packed with childcare, cooking, cleaning and managing a meager household budget while teaching new courses and studying new disciplines: linguistics, anthropology and sociology. I resented his freedom to focus primarily on his studies, but we managed to work out an uneasy collegiality. I even told him how to work in a three-credit course into his load without having to pay additional tuition (there was a flat tuition rate above a certain number of hours). One of the required courses was New Culture and Education in the Southwest, designed as a re-certification requirement for public school teachers. Though full-time students in the doctoral program disdained the course, we had to take it.

"Listen, Rod," I urged. "This class meets on Saturday mornings, and there are no assignments whatsoever—no readings, no papers. This professor just blathers on for three hours. We can get this thing behind us if we can manage to stay awake and look like we're paying attention. Everyone gets an 'A'."

The following Saturday, we both showed up for the course, sitting far across the room from each other where we could not exchange disgusted glances. We sat there, ashamed for all of us and the system that produced this slipshod pretend course, collected our "A" grades, and got back to the hard stuff of anthropology and linguistics.

In my advanced phonology course, students drilled feverishly on sounds and symbols associated with unfamiliar languages such as Chinese and Lithuanian. Professor Bruce's goal was to prepare field anthropologists to record and commit to paper unwritten languages. Graduate students in the program were being prepared to capture the Navajo language as a step toward creating children's textbooks in Navajo. Bernard, the French-Canadian sitting beside me in class, and I decided to practice the sounds and symbols together in preparation for the exam looming formidably in front of us.

We practiced at my place while Amy sat on the living room floor with her crayons and sheaves of newsprint paper. Her red and blue stick figures of girls flashed exuberantly from her page. Bernard and I prepared a huge stack of flashcards and drilled each other over and over as Adam and Bernard covertly sized each other up. They were kindred inhabitants of a different planet, and they recognized that in each other at once.

Bernard, his girlfriend Vera, Adam, and I became friends for the brief period Bernard stayed at the university. Bernard's view of the world, shaped by his amphetamine-laced messianic visions, made it hard for him to focus on the quotidian of mastering the technical aspects of linguistics. Rather, his visions led him to somehow find a fourteen-year-old girl who believed she was an instrument of Edgar Cayce, who by the time of his death in 1945 had become famous for his supposed ability to predict future events. An impressionable girl growing up in a conservative blue-collar home in the suburbs of Albuquerque, she had probably discovered Cayce through her family's membership in the Disciples of Christ Church. Spurred on by Vera and Bernard's avid participation in the little "Cayce cell" circling around the girl, the teenager began to experience more and more apocalyptic visions and to move farther and farther beyond sanity.

One night Adam and I, not having heard from Bernard and Vera for a few weeks, went to visit them at their apartment. When we knocked at the door of the dark apartment, we heard rustling noises from inside. As we turned to leave, Bernard's pale face peered through the glass panel at the side of the door. He opened the door to let us in, casting anxious glances around him. Vera sat on the edge of a sagging couch, dark-circled eyes staring at us warily. A worn-down candle sputtered in the corner of the room. Their teenage prophet had warned them of the imminent end of the world, and they sat waiting in terror for those events to begin.

When the world did not end, the Cayce cell began to disintegrate. The teenage center of the cell had a nervous breakdown, forcing her parents to seek psychiatric help for her. Bernard and Vera broke up. Vera returned to her studies, but Bernard could find no way back. He became increasingly frenetic. He appeared at our house one Saturday.

"Do you have a hammer?" he asked me the moment I opened the door.

"Yes," I responded. "Why do you need a hammer?"

"Just give it to me. I'll bring it back."

I reluctantly handed him the leather-handled hammer my father had given me and watched him rush down the sidewalk and jump into his dilapidated maroon Nash Rambler. I never saw him or the hammer again, but I heard that he was last seen on a remote jungle road in Mexico. His Nash Rambler mired to its axles in mud, he was standing in the middle of the road, arms outstretched in the form of a cross and face turned toward the sky as he screamed, "I am Christ!"

My days in Albuquerque were a mass of contradictions that first year. Feeding the family on $100 a month co-existed with Bernard's apocalyptic visions. Adam's affection for our daughter lived alongside his inability to take care of her. As I engaged in petty jungle warfare with Rod over access to single copies of books, I also found in my coursework exciting ways to think about the diversity and complexity of humans beyond the study of literature. The interdisciplinary structure of my program suited my personality, but the demands on my time gave me scant opportunity to jump in wholeheartedly. My time and energy were pulled in all directions.

The experience of Americans in that year paralleled my own conflicted course. America, too, was pulled in all directions in 1969. Anti-war protests and college student involvement intensified with the vision of the little Vietnamese girl covered with napalm burned on our hearts. On the nightly news, rows of coffins draped with American flags flowed like blood from the mouths of cargo planes, testaments to the toll the war was taking on all of us, supporters and detractors alike.

A sad young veteran in my class told me of lieutenants shot in the back by their troops as they urged them a step too far. The horrors of the My Lai massacre leaked by the press awakened unbelieving Americans to the atrocities committed by our brothers, nephews and sons. Forty-five students were injured and 184 students were arrested at Harvard in a confrontation with police. At one end of the University of New Mexico campus, Eric, the local president of the SDS, his long red hair standing electrically on end, exhorted a small group of students circling cautiously and quizzically around him. At the other end of the campus mall, the American flag standing near the fieldhouse became the rallying point for ROTC students and athletes pushing back against the anti-war effort.

The course I taught as a graduate assistant, The Sociology of Education, was a flashpoint for undergraduates in teacher education. As the course surveyed issues related to ethnicity and class, the students squirmed, encountering the complexity of our society for the first time. Their life experience, as white, mostly middle-class, students had not prepared them to consider the impact of poverty or cultural difference on the way the students learned.

During those times, graduate teaching assistants were thrown into the maw of teaching with no support beyond the provision of a course outline and list of readings. Neither the other grad students nor I were majors in sociology, and we were hardly more prepared than our students for discussing issues presented in the course. In the six years since I'd left my home in Northwest Missouri, I had been immersed in a crash course in living and teaching as an outsider, so it was no surprise to me that the hardest chapter for my students was the one on the Anglo-American culture. They were upset by the very notion that all children did not arrive in school on the first day with the same opportunities and readiness to learn. The concept was alien to their understanding of how "our democracy" was supposed to work. Students from the minority cultures could not absorb the idea that rural poverty existed for some Anglo-Americans; the Anglo students in the class had never considered the possibility that their own opportunities and achievements came to them from an inherited position of social and economic privilege. They believed their work ethic and upright adherence to "American Values" were the sole factors defining their place.

"I'm middle class. Everyone in America is middle class."

"What do you mean 'Anglo-American culture'? This is just our normal stuff. Everyone has these beliefs."

"Everyone wants to be like us. We're the best."

"They're just not trying."

An older woman who had recently returned to college flounced off to the Dean's Office to complain about my "Un-American" reading list on which was a scandalous book that she was being forced to read, *Soul on Ice*. Fortunately for me, the book was not my selection but came from the departmental reading list.

The students' impassioned denials reflected the turmoil ripping through our lives, the accelerating cultural and social changes, the polarizing unwinnable war, and our loss of innocence.

In St. Louis, a man was identified as the first known case of HIV-Aids in the US and a riot at a gay nightclub across the continent ignited the gay rights movement. A son of the most revered political dynasty in America drove his Oldsmobile into the Chappaquiddick and swam away from the night of drunkenness that had led to the drowning death of a pretty staff assistant, that night's casual sexual conquest. At Woodstock, many of the brightest and best from colleges across the country writhed on the pasture grass in an ecstasy of pot and sex, and their horrified parents saw it all on television.

Amid the drama of these events, seemingly small, quiet events were taking place that would upend our ways of being just as much in years to come. Somewhere a semi-conductor company named Intel formed on a highway on the edges of a city in California, Wendy's opened to serve food faster. A little-known family business in Arkansas incorporated as Walmart, and the first ATM was installed in New York City. Ironically, Warner Brothers released its last *Looney Tunes* cartoon, a poignant, accidental commentary on our changing cultural landscape.

I was both removed from the scenes of these tectonic events and immersed in them, each day bracketed by the bills I had to pay, the meals I had to make, the classes I had to teach, the papers I had to write. Adam had enrolled in a geology course as a first step toward getting a college degree. Students had surged into the university that fall, over-filling every popular undergraduate course. Introduction to Geology was the only course available to him for enrollment as a non-degree student, hardly a subject suited to his interests. He floundered at first, having completed high school by getting a high school equivalency diploma during one of his psychiatric incarcerations.

As it turned out, the highly structured, memorization-oriented course was perfect for him. He could master the definitions with the flashcard technique he had watched Bernard and me use. The answers were cut and dried. In that safe, predictable learning environment, he could learn how to study, his paralyzing anxiety and paranoid imaginings of harm held mostly at bay.

Adam memorized those flashcards and found a way to have some purpose in his days. The bright patch in my grinding routine was the bedtime story with Amy as she soaked in every lilting syllable and rhythm, every curve and line in the illustrations, every facet of the story. Our small black and white television had no stand and so sat on the floor at eye level with two-year-old Amy. When Neil Armstrong made his first walk on the moon, his puffy figure looked like the Pillsbury Dough Boy as he bounced weightlessly on the surface of the moon, his leash leading back to a curious pod of metal. Transfixed, Amy stood in her footed pink pajamas and watched him, not sure whether he was a toy or a pet. I envied the astronaut's weightlessness. I felt increasingly mired in shifting sands at the shoreline as high tide rushed inexorably toward me. I stood alone, trying to find solid footing and move to shore.

As the months passed, the shoreline seemed farther and farther away. Overwhelmed with fatigue and sadness at the mess I had gotten myself into, I put one foot in front of the other, day by enervating day. The day after Adam and I had a fight over my desire for a separation, I went to the doctor to find out whether the angry blow Adam had landed on my ear had resulted in a broken eardrum. As I walked to the health center, sounds came to me as if I had held a seashell up to my ear. The eardrum had a tear but was not irretrievably broken. Adam was not a wife-beater, but I had become increasingly wary of his paranoia and impulsivity and tired of knowing that he did not love me. Rather, he needed me to take care of him. I sought out a university counselor.

When I told the counselor, a bored, distant man of fifty-five, he listened to my account of the fight impassively

"So," he said. "Can you forgive him?"

Right. Now it was my job to forgive him. I was the one responsible for fixing the marriage. What about me?

"I suppose."

"I have a four-week group counseling session starting up. Why don't you and Adam join that?"

We joined the group, but as I had suspected, the issues of the couples in this group had little resemblance to ours, which was in a sphere of madness all to itself. After the group sessions had finished, I went to the counselor one more time. This time I felt cornered and desperate enough to lay out the story of our convoluted marriage and my fear and depression in all their painful detail.

I looked at my hands, knotted in my lap, as I revealed my tangled emotions. When I looked up, my face wet, I saw that the counselor had fallen asleep. I walked away, feeling desolately alone, and did not return.

The impetus for having the will to leave the marriage came from an unexpected source. I had made the casual acquaintance of a fellow grad student, Gloria. She was different from me: a breezy, extroverted theater major from a conventional suburban middle-class background. She was smart and confident, warm and people-savvy. One afternoon, she drove me to our house after I had somehow locked myself out and returned to my office to get help. We pried a window open far enough for me to reach the crank and open the window. Removing the screen, she boosted me up through the window and into the house. I opened the door for her, and she waited while I got my keys. She stood silently in the living room, taking in our scant furniture and bare walls.

"This house is the unhappiest house I have ever seen," she finally said. "Its gloom oozes from its pores."

Her direct, unvarnished insight flatly confirmed that the house was an objective correlative of the marriage. Our lives were as sad and dismal as I had thought.

"Yes, I need to get a divorce."

This woman who barely knew me saw in a glance that I needed someone to support me through the separation, and there, from that moment on, anchored me as I took one difficult step after another toward getting out of the marriage. By the end of the spring semester in 1970, Amy and I lived in a slum apartment. It was all I could afford after selling the house and splitting the tiny equity we had accumulated. I tossed in my bed at the apartment, trying to map out surviving the comprehensive exams and dissertation lying ahead. Even with the change to a cheaper place, I could not get us through the month on my graduate assistant paycheck. Beginning that summer, I lacked only two more courses before taking the comprehensive exams and writing the dissertation. I began preparing for the comprehensives but found myself staring at the same page for an hour at a time. I had no memory of anything I had read.

Across town, Adam still sat paralyzed in our house, unable to bring himself to find an apartment and move on. In the crib across our shared bedroom, Amy slept, not knowing or caring that she was about to get a different babysitter. Her current babysitter's idea of taking care of children was to put them on a blanket in front of the television and stuff junk food down their gullets all day long. Amy was too young to put into a pre-school, and I couldn't afford a daycare center.

Jumbled, sleepless nights rolled into days of fruitless attempts to study. I was a gerbil on a treadmill with no apparent jumping-off place. I went to the chair of my department to tell him that I was probably going to have to find a full-time job and leave my graduate teaching post. He was a small man in his late fifties desperately trying to hang on to a youthful image of himself. He wore a natural linen guayabera with a gold Mexican cross hanging from his neck, hoping to offset his receding hairline and myopic eyes framed in gigantic plastic glasses. As I explained that I was in the process of divorcing, his eyes traveled speculatively to my chest and to the top button of my blouse.

"Well," he offered. "I know of a place where you might live. I have a friend who could use a housemate. She...uh...believes in free love, so you'd have to be comfortable with men passing through the house pretty regularly—she lives a different lifestyle, you know."

I got it. Loud and clear.

I imagined my little girl exposed to hairy shirtless men passing by the bedroom door morning and night.

This creep was thinking of adding me to his little "free love" harem.

I couldn't back out of his office fast enough.

Throughout the summer, I struggled for a foothold. My efforts to get a better-paying job in Albuquerque got me nowhere. The academic community and the attractive locale made jobs at my level hard to get. I was over-qualified for high school teaching but under-qualified for the Southwest Research Institute, which asked for—and got—highly experienced, credentialed professionals.

Neither the neighborhood I could afford to live in nor the babysitting situation was good for Amy. My "study paralysis" continued, and I made no progress toward preparing to take my comprehensive exams.

My friends Gloria and Cathy couldn't help me much. Both single women with no children, they insisted that my hooking up with another man was my pathway toward equilibrium. I reluctantly agreed to go with Cathy to a singles group mixer. The rented room at the Holiday Inn was packed with women, their anxious eyes casting nervously around the sterile room to locate the few men surrounded by circles of bolder sisters.

The men strutted and preened, roosters surveying the chicken yard to select the next hen to pounce on. The women surrounding them leaned forward, lips parted and breasts heaving. They laughed too brightly at each banal, witless joke as the men prattled and quipped, unaccustomed to the attention and power they had suddenly been given. An eerily appropriate James Brown song, "Get Up (I Feel Like Being A) Sex Machine," pounded against the sides of the sterile room.

I retreated to the corner of the room, a throbbing headache hovering over my left eye. Cathy hooked up with a flight engineer and jubilantly prepared for a date with him the following weekend. Within a month of beginning to date, nothing was left of the non-start relationship but the herpes she contracted.

Gloria, engaged to marry a successful attorney, looked forward to a prosperous, fulfilling professional life among the old Albuquerque gentry. For her, the solution to my problems was to become romantically involved with John, a friend of ours.

"He's almost finished with his doctorate. He'll be looking around."

"I'm not in the mood to go chasing after some guy."

Something about John made me hesitate. I felt that he had no actual interest in women—that he was either asexual or gay, and I was not attracted to him.

"Just give it a try. I'm having my engagement party next week, and he'll be there."

John and I dutifully sought each other out at the party, both having been lobbied and cajoled by Gloria beforehand. We stumbled and fumbled at trying to find what it was Gloria thought we had in common other than loneliness. We smiled at each other at the end of the evening, silently acknowledging that Gloria's matchmaking had fizzled, both of us relieved that the party was finally over.

The summer was coming to an end, and I had not been able to find a way to get through the next year. It was one of the bitterest moments of my life when I picked up the phone to call my parents and say that I was coming back to Nodaway County, the place I had worked so hard to leave. All I had hoped to become lay in rubble at my feet. I was a broken, exhausted failure with no idea where I could go from there.

I drove eastward with Amy, looking in my rearview mirror to see the turquoise sky and sienna buttes as they receded into the background and finally disappeared. The flat beige wheat fields of western Kansas and then the rolling hills of scorched cornstalks, dry and brown before their time, led me back to where I had begun twenty-eight years earlier.

Ground Zero

The first few weeks on the farm, I sat immobilized in the old oak rocking chair facing the road. I stared unseeing at the distant fence row for an hour at a time, unaware of the passage of time, unable to think. My mother took care of Amy, casting worried glances at me as she lifted Amy to the kitchen counter to involve her in making biscuits. Her legs dangling over the edge of the counter, Amy sat burbling happily with her grandmother as she created horses and cats from the biscuit dough.

As my money began to run out, I forced myself to apply for jobs. Letters came back from area high school principals. "Sorry, you're over-qualified." Destitute or not, I was relieved. If I had been hired to teach in one of the small local schools, I would have felt it was a death sentence; I would never be able to have any semblance of the life I wanted to lead.

After Thanksgiving, I went to Northwest Missouri State to ask Dr. Robbins, still there as English Department chairman, if there were any vacancies. He remembered me from my high school and under-graduate days, telling me that his daughter my age was teaching high school in Kansas City. He related to me as his daughter's classmate, but when I told him I had recently divorced and needed to get a teaching position, his eyes brightened. The infamously lecherous side of him re-appeared.

"Linguistics? Why it happens we do have a vacancy. Can you teach transformational grammar?"

I had taken several linguistics courses, but my teaching experience was in other fields: composition, literature, English as a Second Language and Sociology of Education.

"Well, I haven't done it, but with my recent coursework, I'm sure I could."

We played a game of advance and retreat—he came around the corner of the desk to approach me, and I turned away at the last minute to pick up my purse or read the interim contract he handed me. I backed up toward the door, contract in hand. He enthusiastically wobbled forward on his spindly old legs. We bobbed and danced our way out the door as I signed the contract, returned it to him and made off down the hall with as much grace as I could muster.

Ah. I'd come full circle in more ways than one! The old goat hadn't changed a bit.

The twenty-eight men in the English Department were furious when they heard that I had been hired, guessing correctly that Dr. Robbins had been more dazzled by my figure than by my qualifications for the job. They had assumed that the interim professor currently in the position was a shoo-in for the job. He was one of them. I was not surprised at the male professors' reactions. I was on ground that I did not like, but it was familiar territory. I had a very long road ahead of me to gain their respect, and it was going to be uphill all the way.

I settled for what I could get at the time and began the long process of returning to myself and gaining enough wisdom and calm to get my bearings. Somehow, somewhere I would find a place to stand and, right there in Nodaway County, begin again.

I was scheduled for a final job interview for the tenure-track position with the Vice-President for Instruction. As I stepped across the plush carpet to stand before the vice-president's gigantic walnut desk, I thought he looked like a belligerent little bulldog. A detached piece of me floating in the air smiled that his name was "Dr. Small." His short legs were propped on his desk, a recent copy of *Life* magazine draped across his bullish chest. In his hand was my resume.

"So, I see you have come from the University of New Mexico," he said, looking up at me. "Did you ever take part in any of these protests?"

"No," I lied, hoping my picture was nowhere in the background shots.

He showed me the centerfold photo from the magazine. There was Eric Nelson, the wild-haired radical student body president, grinning full-toothed at me, his curly red hair and antic face huge in the double-spread photo. When Eric, my friend Jennie's lover, had engineered the occupation of the Student Union a few months earlier, Jennie told me about the tactics blow by blow. I had walked to campus to see the silent barricaded Union surrounded by nervous, trigger-happy National Guardsmen.

"This is not going to happen here," said the vice-president, leaning forward and punctuating his words with jabs of his chubby fingers. "If there is one protest, even a food fight in the cafeteria, and I suspect you are involved, I will fire you. There will be no protests or riots at Northwest Missouri State University."

At that moment, I was aware of my long hair and earrings dangling heavily against my shoulders—they were very long for Maryville, Missouri.

My officemates and I squeezed ourselves into cubicles separated only by hastily constructed plywood partitions. We had been hired to teach section after section of English composition to postwar baby boomers and, as a sideline, prove ourselves worthy of tenure in this haven for all-but-dissertation beginning teachers. We needed an academic job, even on a remote outpost, to stay in the game. The gateways to a new generation of tenure-track jobs were rapidly slamming shut. None of us had come to Northwest with the idea of staying there the remainder of our careers, but, in fact, that is what most did. We were the bright, bookish sons and daughters of working-class and farm families, many of us the first in our families to attend college and exemplars of the social stratification of higher education. Ivy League graduate students most often got jobs in Ivy League or top-tier research universities, while graduates from lesser universities more often became faculty in regional universities, a self-perpetuating class system.

Even as assistant professors who had not completed our doctorates, we had credentials from institutions the likes of which Northwest had never seen in such numbers. Northwest was a teachers' college in the process of becoming a regional university, and most of our older colleagues held master's degrees and had taught the same tired courses the same tired ways for decades. My predecessor's ill-concealed arrogance probably cost him his job; as much as Dr. Robbins loved to chase young women, he also leapt (literally) to hire "one of our own." Little did he know how much I, one of the two star English majors of seven years ago, had changed.

As recent Assistant Professor hires, we were the new wave, and we carried that knowledge smugly. We had little respect for the old guys, us Young Turks, but our futures were in their hands.

My officemates greeted me coolly, still mourning that their friend had been passed over for the job I held. They were a boys' club, cruelly disappointed that a young female with a non-traditional degree now resided within their hallowed walls. There were two women and twenty-eight men in the professorial ranks in the department, and the few other women English teachers toiled in perpetuity as composition instructors. I recognized the now-familiar pattern of having to prove my intelligence to the male professors every step of the way.

All winter, I drove between the snow-drifted fence posts toward the farm at the end of the school day. The gray twilight sky blended with the white fields in a moonscape-like terrain, the bleak landscape a mirror of my thoughts. What could I do to survive? I had left the University of New Mexico without my degree, and there were few jobs across the country that year—the ones that were an improvement over the one I had in hand were not going to go to someone with no publications and no doctorate. I had no money and no work experience outside academe. I was a single mother. I was a woman. After Amy went to bed each night, I lay in my girlhood bedroom staring at the ceiling, furious at myself for having gotten myself where I now was, in a box. The cold moon shone relentlessly through the window of the unheated room, unblinking. I could not sit frozen like a terrified rabbit in the road. I had to move forward in some direction.

As a first step, I needed to leave my parents' home and function as an adult. Maryville had no apartments suitable for children in 1971—only run-down second-story student housing, and I had no money to buy a house. In the spring, I borrowed $4,000 from my father to buy a mobile home—not my idea of beauty and grace but paid for. I could save money for a down payment on a house. The mobile home park sprawled treeless across a barren hillside that had been a corn-field two years earlier. A friend and I crossed a field to cut branches of willow from the banks of a creek to sprout in the muddy expanse outside the mobile home. As my friend, Amy, and I walked across the field with our willow branches, I saw a herd of pigs charging down the hill toward us. Visions of pigs stomping Amy into a bloody mass on the ground galvanized me. Wielding the eight-foot branch in front of me like a broadsword, I screamed a rebel yell and charged the startled pigs. They stopped stock still and stared at me. What was this crazy woman doing? They had only been running excitedly toward us in anticipation of their evening feeding. I saw how ludicrous my charge had been, and I laughed for the first time in many months. My ability to laugh and my fierce mother instinct were intact, and my will to fight had begun to kick in.

I drove the English professors crazy from the beginning. They shared the philosophy that the only content freshman composition students should write about was literature (spell that "Lit-ra-tyur"), and the only way to improve their writing was to give them targeted exercises from the hefty grammar handbook they had unanimously adopted. Homer, who currently served as the rotating chair of the composition program, believed all women should be like his sweet, docile wife Denise and obey the cardinal rule of English Department Law: following the departmental syllabus with no deviation. My study of language pedagogy and linguistics and my own teaching of nontraditional students had convinced me of the wrong-headedness of the department's unquestioning adherence to tradition. They wanted to teach literature, not composition, out of their own selfish interest. Composition was "women's work," and they were made for finer scholarly things.

Homer had heard that I was teaching material outside the specifications of the departmental syllabus. He decided that the way to handle this subversiveness was to convene a "committee" of teachers, of whom I was to be one, to go over the syllabus and re-affirm its validity and the efficacy of the textbooks for the course. The meeting was not going well, as the committee pored over the syllabus line by line without comment from me. He asked us to take a break. As I stood in the corridor by the water fountain, I discovered that the men's voices were bouncing off their restroom walls, and I could hear every word. They were strategizing about how to handle me. I listened to their conversation, realizing that there was no opportunity for me to have a similar conversation with anyone in the women's room.

Back in committee, they took their turns justifying the syllabus and providing mutual support for their views. I had thought through the points they planned to make and, with cheerful detachment, demolished each unexamined assumption or bit of received wisdom as it came up. It was not going to win me any friends, but I was too angry at their clumsy machinations to care. They left the session stewing in frustration but not quite so eager to proclaim their opinions as gospel.

Knowing that Homer lay in wait for me, I took care to use assignments laid out in the syllabus but could not resist sprinkling them with exercises reflecting my own philosophy. One morning I went into the English Department office early to mimeograph the day's lesson plan. I sleepily fit the mimeograph stencil into the machine's bracket and began to make copies when I realized that I had put the stencil onto the shiny steel cylinder upside down. The unauthorized exercises were printed distinctly on the cylinder. I had ten minutes to go before Homer would come into the office, so I frantically scrubbed the surface of the machine with Kleenex, finishing the clean-up just as he came through the door.

"Good morning," I said brightly as I scooped up the offending exercise sheets and briskly left for class.

Homer's term as composition chair was over, and Dr. Robbins was retiring, so I was spared the ax that I was, in so many ways, asking for. I could not bring myself to become a "better fit" for the place I was in and to accept the gender role that I was supposed to take in that backwater bastion of male academics, but if I was going to survive there, I was going to have to find ways to fill a niche in the department and blunt the animus toward me. The other woman in the department gave me a heavy brass key ring impudently stamped with the words "Executive Toilet" as we made a pact to not let ourselves be vanquished by the bland-faced, petty scholars threatening to soundlessly flush our academic ambitions down the toilet like unwanted goldfish.

I was in new territory as I began to pick my way through the razor blade-strewn path to becoming a college professor. Throughout my graduate studies, both at the University of Kansas and the University of New Mexico, I never had a woman professor other than a visiting professor from Yeshiva University who flew into Albuquerque three times a semester to lecture in Psycholinguistics. The idea of encouraging or mentoring women graduate students was not yet a glimmer in anyone's eye—in 1970, only 11 percent of full professors nationwide were female. The general view was that professors would be wasting their valuable time on encouraging women who would (and should) just get married and perform as the bright wifely satellite of an aspiring young male professor.

Having such an uneasy seat in the English Department, I found my friends among young professors in other departments. We were bound together by our intention to get out of Maryville and by our hunger for the cultural environment of major universities. At our Saturday night gourmet dinners, we lamented the dearth of theater, concerts and lectures. We formed an island to ourselves. The trapped faculty wives in the group tried to start art galleries and bookstores, desperately hoping to find a way to cope. All their attempts to bring university-like enterprises to the town sputtered and died. Another tippled her way to oblivion in the kitchen as she pored over her Julia Child cookbook and created elaborate meals of Escargots Provençale and Boeuf Bourguignon.

Jason's wife, Stephanie, created a sensation in the community by nonchalantly mentioning in an interview about her painting that she and Jason were humanists. For weeks, angry hang-up calls bounced off the walls of their artistically decorated house. Townsmen stared unbelievingly at Stephanie as she wore her paint-spattered overalls downtown to shop for the art supplies that were never there.

Our children suffered on the playground because their parents were "different," and they had to find their own ways to fit in—by slavishly conforming to peer styles and language or by rebelling against authority. One day my daughter said to me in exasperation, "Mother, can't you just wear an apron and make cookies? My friend Jamie wants to come to our house after school and look in our refrigerator. She wants to see what capers look like."

Sometimes these faculty kids resorted to mischief. One hot day in May, some professors' kids, bored and looking for an outlet, hacked into their school's computer and locked all the grades up. They created mayhem as school officials desperately looked for ways to unlock the computer and determine who was eligible to graduate.

Their professor parents continued to look for ways to escape, and if they couldn't make their getaway, they tried to build their resumes and advance at Northwest. When the new department chair came to the college, he wanted to appoint a director of Freshman Composition to manage the burgeoning number of freshmen coming to college, and I was horrified to learn that the inexperienced chairman was about to appoint Morty Bly, one of the weakest members in the department— no questions asked.

"I understand you're thinking of appointing Morty Bly as Director of Freshman Comp," I blurted out the minute I entered the chairman's office. "You are about to make a mistake. Have you looked at his teacher evaluations? Complaint after complaint—the lowest in the department, but don't believe me—go look for yourself. I understand, too, that you want to make some changes in the way composition is taught here, to modernize the department. Bly has no relevant coursework or past interest in composition and rhetoric. He does not publish in the field—or any other, for that matter. He doesn't go to conferences. He has no record at all."

Dr. Carlson stared at me, embarrassed. I was right. In his first job as a department chairman, he was walking into making a big mistake because he hadn't done his homework. Our relationship as friends and colleagues developed from there based on our mutual need to succeed and recognition that we would be telling each other truths, as we saw them, for a long time.

A few weeks later, he had done his homework, discovering that what I had told him was true. In our next conversation, he asked, "What would you do if you were director?"

"I would establish a college writing center, create a developmental writing course based on the latest research for underprepared students, and establish a placement process based on student writing samples rather than invalid grammar test scores."

I was appointed to the position, much to the chagrin of the male literature professors. In a way, Dr. Carlson made his second mistake in appointing me because he had to defend me from professorial attacks again and again as I set about to do exactly what I had promised to do. As the new programs and courses came to being, the stature of the department rose in the eyes of the administration and professors in other departments who had longed for more effective writing courses.

I learned to use hard data in reports to the faculty senate and work campus-wide with professors. I sought out professors in other departments and counselors as partners in research and publishing projects.

Dr. Carlson warned me that I would need to complete my doctorate to get tenure. A friend offered to go with me to New Mexico and watch over my six-year-old while I took my last two courses, Statistics and Language Disorders. On a hot June day in 1973, my car loaded down with my daughter, a German Shepherd, my colleague, and camping gear, I headed for Albuquerque, the car radio blaring news of the Watergate scandal while Amy plugged in her earphones and listened to her tape of *The Fiddler on the Roof* for the fiftieth time.

Albuquerque blazed hot against the roof of the loaded, swaying white Pontiac as we drove around the campus area looking for an apartment. The landlords took one look at the German Shepherd and the child in the back seat and refused to rent me an apartment for the summer—short-term leases, a dog and a kid were sure trouble. Four partying law students seemed like a better gamble. We drove to a campground on the West Mesa at the edge of the city and pitched our tent, looking carefully around our site for rattlesnakes.

The next morning, I peered anxiously into the campground's dull restroom mirror, hoping to get my make-up on straight and look like a credibly serious graduate student rather than a sand-dusted camper from the Sixties. I had an appointment with the new dean of the department whom I had never met. At least Lecherous Larry, the former dean, had moved on.

"Why are you here?"

I heard the chill in his voice.

"I want to finish my coursework this summer and move toward completion of the degree."

"Let me see your coursework." His eyebrows bunched together over the top of his big plastic glasses as he stared in disgust at the list.

"Why this is a hodge-podge of unrelated courses. How can you possibly think this constitutes a degree program?" He handed the paper back to me as if it were a rumpled used Kleenex.

I could see two years of study and tenure going up in smoke and heard the all too familiar disdain in the voice of the male-academic-in-power.

"I think you'd better look again. My advisor when I was here is now the Dean of the Graduate School and we picked those courses with inter-disciplinary study in mind. He would be interested to know that these courses are now unacceptable. Further, if you read the list carefully, you will see that I have fulfilled each of your own department's requirements, category by category, in accordance with the catalog under which I was admitted. Under your own department's guidelines, I have two more courses to complete, and I am here for your signature so that I can enroll in them."

I stared unblinkingly into his newly cautious brown eyes and handed the enrollment form to him. He quickly signed it, and I stalked out, still burning with fury. With adrenalin still raging in my brain, I drove back to the campground.

I flung my textbooks into the tent.

"I'm going to live in this tent for the summer, and I am going to take those two courses. I've had it. C'mon, Amy, let's go to the recreation center to cool off and play some ping-pong. This is where we are going to be until August."

For a week, we sweat through the late afternoon heat. The owner of the campground noticed the little girl and the dog making daily rounds on the campground trails and the small tent drooping forlornly against the dry, parched mesa as I swatted bugs off my sweating arms and legs and tried to study.

"I have a trailer house up the hill that you could rent."

We planted a little cactus garden a few feet from the wrought-iron steps at our front door. Amy watered them faithfully every day and watched them begin to bloom in brilliant red and yellow as the endless revelations from the Watergate hearings rolled through the flimsy aluminum trailer house door. I spent as little time as possible on campus, always filled with guilt and anxiety over leaving Amy and my friend to fill the long hot afternoons while I was in class.

When I returned to Northwest that fall, I faced a daunting set of tasks—passing prelims and writing a dissertation, gaining enough acceptance in the English Department to get tenure, fulfilling the required professional and service components for advancement through the ranks and merit raises, teaching four to five classes a semester, raising a daughter, coping with my sense of being trapped in Maryville—and staying sane. Summers were easier than winters. I interspersed work on the doctorate with getting in touch with the part of me that gains strength from the land and working with my hands.

I found solid old dressers and tables at country auctions and refinished them under the spreading mulberry in my backyard. When the tomatoes weighed down my parents' tomato vines in August, I canned spaghetti sauce for winter suppers. My sister and I drove to back fencerows and woods we knew about to forage for bittersweet, mushrooms, and redbud saplings. My brother liked to hunt deer better than he liked to eat them, so I canned and froze the venison he brought me. In early spring, the smell of the warm soil restored my spirit after a long school year as Amy and I went to my parents' farm on Saturdays to help plant the peas and onions.

I lived in Missouri, enjoying and, yes, enduring a parallel existence as a college professor in town during the week and a country daughter most Sunday mornings. Every October or November, Mom and I made mincemeat together to use in pies and cookies during the cold winter months ahead. We felt close as we talked together over the chopping of the apples and nuts and the grinding of the roast beef with the old metal meat grinder clamped to the end of the kitchen table. It was a time for me to take a break from grading compositions and reading for the next week's classes. It was a time for her to share with me a vanishing practice. Together we inhaled the scents of cinnamon, vinegar and cloves permeating the raisins and nuts on those fall days. Amy passed through the kitchen, enjoying the quiet talk and spicy scents, as she made her way out the back door to kick her way through piles of red and yellow leaves or climb the ancient apple tree one more time before winter. Most of the time, my life as a professor and my life as a native of Nodaway County did not intersect.

On weekdays, I entered the campus fray. I preferred campus-wide committee work to the intense, conflicted business of the English Department. Because no one in the department respected the campus-wide Faculty Senate or wanted to be bothered by it, the department's senator was chosen on a rotational basis, so the professors were happy to give me a turn and, with my doctor's degree finally completed, I could handle the time commitment. My campus involvement brought me in contact with one of the most amazing women I ever met, Irene Hammond. While I had no mentor for threading my way through the English Department, Irene taught me how to get difficult things done without being killed.

Irene was the university registrar who had begun her career as a campus secretary. She had earned her position by becoming indispensable and by learning how to assert herself without threatening the administrators' notions of femininity. They trusted her no-nonsense, motherly farm-wife demeanor. Underneath it all, she was made of steel. We got to know each other when she enlisted me to help write the university's first affirmative action plan, which the administration hoped would never reach completion. They were very comfortable with systematically underpaying women faculty and letting them languish in the lower faculty ranks. Week by week, Irene and I marched relentlessly through drafting the plan. Irene taught me how to maneuver the document through endless consultations and revisions, carefully laying the groundwork to get the plan approved. We listened with straight faces to the Vice President for Student Services explain to us why the male janitors should get higher wages than the female admissions clerks, all of whom held associate degrees.

"Having to clean the toilets in the restrooms is more stressful. The janitors need to get more."

Irene and I, who regularly cleaned toilets at home, didn't blink an eye, but we acquired the comparative data from other colleges to silence him. I learned several other tactics—parliamentary procedure, strategic committee assignments, timing and whipping votes, campus-wide networking—in my time as senator and gradually became a campus leader.

The university's Faculty Senate was an ineffectual faculty governance body, and the administration counted on the senators' inertia to make changes such as the elimination of weak or redundant minors. One spring afternoon, the senate president and the dean of instruction brought, with no supporting documentation, a motion to abolish several minors in the Humanities. They had innocuously posted the documentation and held a hearing on a balmy Friday afternoon several weeks earlier, knowing that the documentation would go unread and the hearing unattended.

Predictably, the senators asked no questions and voted two minors out.

"I don't feel comfortable with what we're doing. I know if I were in the position of my fellow faculty members in Humanities, I would feel sad to see us rubber-stamping motions that destroy their department. I don't feel that I can vote on this motion because I didn't read the material before this meeting, and I didn't attend the hearing. I didn't act responsibly as a senator. I don't know whether these minors should be removed because I haven't done my homework."

Smiling disarmingly at the infuriated dean, I moved to table the motion to give due respect to the Humanities faculty and to honor our own positions as senators. By tabling the motion, the programs couldn't be removed in time to be omitted from the next published class schedule or the college catalog. The next morning the chair of the Humanities Department, a crony of the literature professors, appeared in the English Department office.

"You know, I never thought I liked her, but I have to now say, 'She's all right.'"

The women assistant professors in the Speech and English Departments had begun to meet for lunch off-campus to support each other as we tried to navigate through our departments' politics. As a pat on our pretty little heads, the university approved our use of campus facilities to sponsor Women's Week activities. We decided to make our points through skits, lampooning the notion of the day that all women needed to do to succeed was to be more like men. One of us dressed in a flowery pastel dress with glitzy bangles dangling from her wrists; the other dressed in a dark, pinstriped mannish suit and severely tailored stiff white shirt.

Clearly, John Molloy, author of *The Woman's Dress for Success Book*, would put his money on the woman in the suit: "As I pointed out, the best garment for a woman to wear is generally the skirted suit. But to some Midwesterners the skirted suit represents the pushy Eastern woman. Don't give up your suit; it will help you much more than it will hurt you. But when you are going to be dealing with someone who might have a negative reaction to a high-authority suit, you can shift to a suit in a softer color." In the skit, the woman in the flowered dress emerged as a hard-bargaining woman with her head on straight; the woman in the "high-authority suit" was an idiot mannequin. We were highly doubtful that wearing a skirt suit would get us anywhere at Northwest.

Our humor wasn't getting us anywhere either. The men who blocked our way day after day didn't come to the skit, but, also, at the head of the phalanx of men determined to preserve their rightful dominant position was the dean of instruction. As we watched the dean promote, tenure and inequitably pay mediocre professor after professor while we waited for our turns, we became angrier and angrier. One night over a glass (or two) of wine, we distributed among ourselves some little Guatemalan trouble dolls, promising to express our anger through poking our dolls below the belt with pins while incanting the dean's name at six o'clock on Sunday nights. Not one of us believed in voodoo, but we needed a way to vent our frustration.

After about a month of our dark ritual, we heard on a Monday morning that the dean had just had emergency surgery for a blocked colon. We surreptitiously sought each other out in the halls—what if he died? We were sobered at the thought of what our anger could do.

The dean lived and continued to protect his men. One of the dean's faculty friends used the Faculty Senate's committee selection process to become, year after year, the chairman of the Affirmative Action Committee charged with the implementation of the plan. This friend, then, never called a meeting of the group together. To stop him, I maneuvered to get an appointment to the committee on committees knowing that a friend of mine, the geology professor chairing the committee, would help remove him. The committee's job was to look at each faculty member's list of committees he or she would be willing to serve on; true to form, the dean's little helper designated Affirmative Action as his first choice, and, with his own ironic sense of humor, he named the Cap and Gown Committee as his second choice. He vainly believed that a full professor of his self-proclaimed stature would never be assigned to the most laughable, useless committee on campus, but it happened. I had taken Irene's velvet bulldozer lessons to heart.

The five women in our group decided to take the legal route and drove to Kansas City to file an Affirmative Action complaint against the university for failing to even pretend that it was implementing its Affirmative Action plan.

"You have an excellent case," said the case manager, "but you realize that once this case is filed, all of your witnesses' statements along with their names will be made public."

"Yes. We are willing to go ahead."

The case manager squirmed in his chair, looking down at his hands.

"I have to tell you—in confidence—that you might want to think again. President Reagan has directed our office to drag our feet on these complaints—this will go on for years with the administration knowing who you and your witnesses are."

We couldn't put our untenured colleagues—male and female—through the treatment that would await them—and us, and now knew the political climate was going to be impossible for years, even decades, to come. The women's rights movement had been mortally wounded by silent assassins in their Washington, DC, offices. If those of us who wrote the complaint were able to sit down together twenty years later, we would have noted ruefully that the number of women in the professoriate had not moved and that an insidious dual system of adjunct and nontenure-track contract faculty, overwhelmingly female, and tenure ranks, predominantly male, was firmly in place—the universities' solution to never-ending legislative budget cuts. We trudged on, begrudgingly given tenure. Rather than feeling elated, I felt more stuck in place than ever.

In addition to my work as Director of Freshman Composition and the newly formed Writing Center, I was charged with the creation of an English as a Second Language program as the university sought to get its share of international students flooding colleges nationwide. Most of our students came from Iran, their parents having sent them for safety from the warring factions tearing apart their country following the fall of the Shah of Iran. Our program swelled with students from the four major factions. Some spoke English fluently, others not a word. The class sessions were surreal. Mastering a second language was the least of the students' concerns; every class was filled with anxious students worried about their families at home and fearful and mistrusting of each other.

Four of my students, three brothers and a sister, were the children of one of the four generals executed summarily when the Shah's regime fell. Their father had foreseen the danger they would be in and remembered Northwest Missouri State, a university in the vicinity of Fort Leavenworth, where he had received military training. He sent them to Northwest for their safety. A few weeks after the general's execution, his daughter called me at midnight one night.

"We're leaving. I can't tell you where we are going, but we have to go."

And then they were gone.

It was impossible to engage the remaining depressed, terrified students in learning. Each day we faced dejected, uncommunicative, unprepared students in our offices as they came to beg to be passed so they could stay in the country. As I sat in my windowless office on a spring morning, three agitated Kurdish students, two men and a woman, stood blocking the office door.

"You have to pass her. If you don't pass her, she will have to go home and may be killed." Fatima, her hennaed red hair cropped short, stared at me and moved her hand to her bulging coat pocket.

Did she have a gun?

I knew the students were right—a militant female Kurd striding mannishly in her Levis would never be allowed to move freely in the newly formed theocratic country intent on pushing all women back into burqas and enforced cloistering. I had to take the chance that she did not have a gun because if I passed her, I would have to pass them all. Floods of refugee students would get word and come to the college. The students kept secrets about themselves from each other, but they were united in their desire to discover how to work the American college system, and, about that, there were no secrets.

"I can't do it."

I took in a breath only when I saw their shoulders drop dejectedly as they turned to leave. This psychological showdown with an undercurrent of potential violence was the first of my career, but not the last. The turmoil in the Middle East was only beginning to come to American shores. I have never forgotten Fatima or the general's daughter and have wondered if they managed to survive the maelstrom that had caught them in its furious swirl.

By the end of the semester, the Iranians had found the hole in the fence of the American college system. Thirty miles north of the university, a struggling junior college welcomed them with open arms—the students streamed northward to a place having no entrance requirements, no inconvenient visa policies or tiresome academic standards. They had found a place to hide while they waited for calmer days in Iran.

As a trickle of students from the Middle East and Africa came to live in Maryville, the college administrators were slow to understand that the students and surrounding community were not prepared to deal with their cultural differences. The community's racial anger churning beneath the surface was about to spill over. The dean of students, a local farm boy made good, went about his work as usual, retiring to his acreage on weekends to tend his little garden farmer crops; his resident assistants in the men's dorms followed their practice of going home to surrounding small towns on weekends.

When a Nigerian student was charged with minor assault after having been heckled by white students in the dorm, the dean of students decided that the best way to protect the Nigerian and defuse the racial and ethnic tensions in the dorm was to advise authorities to sentence the Nigerian to two weekends in jail. One of these weekends fell on June 6 in the summer term of 1983. On Saturday night, the jailer checked on Wallace Nduka Morgan and the other men in the unlocked jail cells; as soon as he left, Rodney A. Pankau, one of the local bad boys jailed with four others for disorderly conduct at a bar, proposed "a blanket party" for Morgan. The men launched their unprovoked attack on Morgan, beating his head and chest and kicking him with their cowboy boots as he screamed and cried for help. No one heard him. He crawled back to his cell and died there after a second beating. He was discovered there only after the jailer ambled, scratching and yawning, into his cell the next morning.

I did not know Wallace Morgan personally, but as a faculty member who worked closely with international students, I was sickened and enraged at the university officials' silence and paralysis. I organized protests, and faculty and staff joined me in demanding an investigation. Two days into the protests, the vice-president for student affairs summoned me. I was one of a group of faculty considered to be on the outspoken fringe in this regional university composed largely of first-generation college professors trying to finish their PhDs and move on or home-grown faculty who, between their ears, had never left their Northwest Missouri roots. I was hired on the presumption that I was one of those locals who would fit right into the community and never rock the boat. Both the administration and I were having trouble fitting me into that category.

I wondered if Vice-President Small waited in the office with Jeff, his student affairs counterpart. Jeff was a tall handsome ex-basketball player, his friendly smile, genial personality, and blond good looks having promoted him to his station at a young age. On this day, he met me alone, looking pale and nervous.

"Why are you doing this? We have trouble enough right now. We could not have known what would happen down there. Herb was just trying to keep him safe for the weekend."

Jeff was more frightened than I was.

"Channel our energy. Take the rage of the protestors and turn it into something that could help you."

I don't know where my idea came from—certainly I had not thought of it before the meeting—but I advised him to form a joint task force to investigate campus safety, ask for recommendations with a quick turn-around, personally face the task force and listen with interest, implementing as many of the ideas as he could.

As the task force worked, federal investigators came to town, and the four men were charged with capital murder. The hearings and trials ground on for two years with Pankau finally convicted, not for murder but manslaughter, and sentenced to only fifteen years in prison. Some positive changes at the university did occur, but for the larger community, the murder was an outburst of drunken hooligans on a hot summer weekend and only that. The community saw no connection between the murder and the community's deep-rooted violent, racist history still seething beneath the surface after the notorious lynching four miles from my childhood home fifty years earlier. My life as a professor and my life as a local's daughter intersected. I wanted out of there.

This grotesque act of violence did not garner as much international attention as the vigilante execution of Ken McElroy in Skidmore, a town of 280 people, two years earlier. Both events intertwined with my dual life as an "outsider" academic and daughter of the community. While the Nigerian student's murder took place within the sphere of my academic life, McElroy's violent saga played out in the country roads and towns where my parents still lived, seven miles away. My father and my brothers knew McElroy. His brother Marvin, after all, lived on the farm next to my parents.

I first knew of Ken McElroy when Joel, a mild-mannered Philosophy professor in the office next to me, told me that his wife Anne was being stalked by the notorious Skidmore bully. Anne, a beautiful, fiery woman of thirty, was assistant district attorney and was galvanizing the DA's office to pursue McElroy more aggressively, his having avoided conviction for charges brought against him twenty-one times in twenty years. McElroy's attorney in Kansas City was allegedly connected to the mob, and time after time, witnesses refused to take the stand, taking seriously McElroy's threats to burn their homes. According to court records, McElroy raped a girl of twelve and impregnated her. After the girl and another of his captive lovers fled his house and returned to her girlhood home, he found the two girls and forced them back to his home. He then returned to her parent's house when they were gone, killed the family dog and burned down their house. The district attorney's office was preparing to finally get him convicted as Anne and Joel left for work each morning, knowing he was the hulking figure in the car across the street. McElroy had recently shot the owner of a Skidmore grocery store in the neck because an employee accused a McElroy child of stealing candy.

When I went to visit my parents that weekend, I asked about the increasingly violent bully. My father laughed a little nervously.

"Oh, he won't bother us. One day Ken drove in here and visited a while. He said to me, 'You won't have any trouble. You're all right. You've always been good to Marvin.'"

Marvin and his wife Grace had even gone on a trip to California with Mom, Dad, and me thirty years earlier, when I, at age twelve, slouched down in the back seat of the car. I inwardly rolled my eyes all the way across the Mojave Desert while Grace detailed the condition of her bowels "what with all the strange food on the road." My parents always said Marvin was "the nicest man around, always trying to make up for his brother's orneriness."

A few Saturdays later, Ken McElroy drove into Skidmore to buy a six-pack of beer. The county sheriff was in town that morning meeting with residents. His advice to them was to form a neighborhood watch to gain protection from the bully's intensifying belligerence. When a man ran into the meeting to tell the gathering that McElroy was in town, the sheriff got in his car and sped away. Despairing to get protection for their families, neighborhood men shot and killed McElroy on the street in front of more than forty witnesses. McElroy was shot in the head through the rear window of the car as he sat in his Silverado, preparing to back out of his parking space with the six-pack of beer he had just bought. His massive weight slumped on the steering wheel as he bore down on his accelerator. The engine, still in neutral gear, screamed under the pressure of McElroy's dying foot while someone opened the passenger door and dragged his young wife to safety in the nearby bank building.

No one in the village saw anything, and no one would offer witness testimony. Whether a few residents in town that day grabbed their guns on impulse or the event was a planned vigilante event, the people in the community closed ranks, relieved that the bully was finally gone from their lives. "Gun Justice" had been part of the area's history from its beginning. The district attorney declined to file charges against anyone, and though my brother, who had married his Skidmore sweetheart, was told privately who pulled the trigger, he couldn't remember anything either. My parents' neighbors, Marvin and Grace, sold their farm and moved to a mobile home retirement village in Texas, hoping no one remembered the name "McElroy" or that Saturday morning when gunfire suddenly erupted in Skidmore, Missouri.

Although I had made a place for myself at the college, my dissatisfaction increased. The entrenched conservatism of the university's culture, the community's violence and stagnation were going to pull me under. As Walmart moved in, independent businesses and any small-town charm Maryville had ever enjoyed evaporated. Main Street Maryville died, except for student-oriented bars, laundromats and pizza parlors wedged between empty storefronts. Wilcox, the village next to my parents' farm, had lost its original inhabitants, replaced by renters who took over the crumbling houses fronted by broken-down motorcycles and rusty cars.

I had no romance in my life, and there were no available men in Maryville. Though my libido was far from dead, the sordid invitations of a couple of the married men in my department saddened and disgusted me. Amy, too, needed a change. Already a perceptive reader, astute observer and gifted writer, she did not fit the small-town conformist mold of many classmates. I wanted her to have a chance to find a setting better matched to her spirit, and that heightened my desire to leave. My friends, also having completed their doctorates or retrained for other work, positioned themselves to leave. It was time to go.

The climate was poor for getting another college teaching position in English. Most tenure-track positions were now filled by professors in my age group with no intentions of moving, and part-time teaching exploded. I turned to applying for a Fulbright to improve my credentials but, even more, to escape the place that was harder and harder to bear. When the offer to serve as a junior Fulbright lecturer in Yugoslavia came, I seized it. Amy and I spent the year in Osijek, a small Croatian city in the center of the country.

Our studio apartment perched like an ugly crow's nest on the fourteenth floor of a grim, gray, brutally austere Communist-era building. Within the confines of that tiny apartment, we would have a metamorphosis, bursting out of our silken threads to fly. Amy registered in high school correspondence courses from the University of Nebraska so that she would keep pace with her class while living abroad. Each morning after I set off for the two-mile walk to the college, Amy was faced with completing lessons in literature, algebra and history on her own. She'd always been more interested in her role as class clown than in doing homework and attaining good grades. A gifted mind, she rebelled against the bland, rote classes and teachers she'd been exposed to in Maryville. Now the burden of self-discipline and self-directed learning was primarily on her, and she became a good student.

We made some failed attempts to find age-mates for her to get to know, but a physically well-developed young teenager from America had little in common with girls her age in Osijek. These girls were pre-pubescent, hiding shyly behind their mothers. Dressed in little white ankle socks, patent leather shoes and lacy white dresses, they looked and acted like children far younger than Amy. The college freshmen I taught turned out to be good matches for her. Almost every night, she went out on "The Corso" with them to stroll up and down the broad avenue, cruising, eating ice cream and meeting up for group dates. The students, far from their eavesdropping Communist teachers, felt safe to ask Amy questions about government systems in the United States. Amy, who had never cared one way or the other about American government, suddenly needed to understand and explain topics such as "representative government" and the Voting Rights Act.

She and her friends attended the movie *Ordinary People* starring Mary Tyler Moore. From their scornful, scandalized remarks, she came to understand that what we Americans saw as a realistic depiction of an upper-middle-class American family's private sorrow was, for the Croatian viewers, an affirmation of the decadence of American capitalist society. The government only permitted American movies to be shown that showed Americans and their capitalist system in a negative light. When the college was not in session, we traveled to Greece, Italy, Hungary, Germany and Austria. Amy's worldview expanded exponentially.

For me, I felt I had been released from a stifling box. Our daily lives were challenging as we endured the long lines caused by food shortages, power outages and bans on coffee importation alongside the Croats. For Amy's birthday dinner, I went to three different markets, walking six miles, and stood in line for an hour and a half to get a small box of strawberries. On Tuesday nights, when our heat and light were turned off by officials conserving energy, we visited friends or sat in the sputtering light of cheap candles on the fourteenth floor. The worst fate on those nights was to be in the elevator of the high-rise when the power outage began its four-hour stint at an unpredictable time. To avoid this possibility, we climbed the fourteen flights of stairs on Tuesdays.

These hardships were not debilitating—we, after all, endured them only temporarily and to a much lesser degree because, in that society, my Fulbright salary defined us as rich. The privations were not life-limiting, and, in that unfamiliar cultural terrain, they illuminated the class and ethnic differences in the country. Our friendship with a Croatian family deepened our immersion in the culture. On weekends, Bojan, folk editor of the local newspaper, took us into the Lipizzaner stables and farm homes of the countryside, introducing us to the dances, Sunday dinners, pig killings and needlework of the rural Croatians.

It took a while for us to figure out that we, because of this association with the Croatian family, were shunned by the Serbian professionals in the city. By political design, Tito had placed members of the major Yugoslavian ethnicities in each other's regions to try to build a national Yugoslavian identity; as events a few years later would show, the experiment did not work. In the college where I taught, the teachers were Serbian, and the local teachers' college students were Croatian. We were invited to a social gathering of a Serbian only to be unceremoniously dropped the following week by our hosts. Our apartment was bugged, so we learned to converse on any matter of possible interest to anyone on walks outside the building. The Senior Fulbright scholar and I read long involved recipes with exotic ingredients to each other over the phone, creating countless hours of work for the translators tasked with transcribing our phone calls.

The Serbian chair of the English Department drew a line on my gradebook and indicated how many students I should fail in my courses according to their relative standing in the class. At Northwest, such intrusion into my classroom (and I had experienced some of those in Maryville) would have plunged me into a depression. In Yugoslavia, they appalled me, but I saw them through the lens of a person only passing through, and I would act according to my conscience. Because there were no English-language textbooks, I was expected to laboriously type out and then mimeograph the lessons for my five classes a day with a couple of outdated resources available in their meager library. Realizing that I could never keep that pace and that the methods proposed (drill and practice exercises) would not increase my students' fluency, I chose another path. A trip to the American Embassy in Belgrade yielded gifts of hundreds of textbooks for the college; my preferred method of instruction was live practice with using the language.

The students and I sang Beatles songs together. Students gave speeches demonstrating how to do something they knew well after watching me model the assignment by making Snickerdoodles. We talked about bumper stickers and T-shirt slogans until I found out they were politically dangerous to teach because they sometimes expressed political opinions or derided American political leaders, practices unheard of in the Yugoslavia of 1980. When I left the college at the end of the year, I don't think the department chair was at all unhappy to see me go, but I didn't care. The next year my students were recognized as being the most advanced English language speakers at their grade level in the country's college competitions.

The most difficult challenge for us was the daily, culturally sanctioned sexual harassment which dogged us from our first day to our last day in Yugoslavia. The orientation crash course the Fulbright Commission sponsored for us in Belgrade never touched upon what we would face as women alone. When Amy and I left the Belgrade airport on our first day, Amy was exhausted and doubled over with anxiety and air sickness. All the signage was written in the Cyrillic alphabet. The usual cabs driven by industry-regulated, multi-lingual drivers did not exist.

"Take the bus," we were told at the information desk. "It's right outside and only a couple of miles to your hotel."

As we entered the bus filled solely with men, the calls, challenging taunts, and lewd hand gestures began immediately. Faced with more than twenty laughing, yelling men, I thought Amy and I might be gang-raped. I demanded that the bus driver stop and unload our bulging suitcases from the belly of the bus. The men shouted at us from the bus windows, seeming to be asking us to get back on, that we would be all right. I stubbornly, angrily shook my head and waved the bus driver on with a vehemence I did not feel. I could see the hotel in the distance. Block by block, Amy and I could drag our suitcases to it, a safer choice than riding with those hormone-crazed men.

We learned later that any women traveling alone, especially at night, were subjected to that treatment, the belief being that women alone in trains or buses were prostitutes. The prospect of having a young beautiful American girl like my daughter was deliciously irresistible, and a woman eating alone in a restaurant was fair game. I could not eat lunch at a restaurant between classes without looking up to see a man using obscene hand gestures to invite me to have sex. I had to learn to keep my eyes down in public places to avoid these encounters. If a light bulb in the sixteen-foot-high ceilings of our apartment needed changing, the maintenance man had to change the bulb above the watchful, scowling stare of his wife. A man could not be trusted to control himself around a woman alone, it seemed. If our travels took us on night trains, we could expect to be unable to use the bathrooms or leave our train compartment without drunken male bodies pressing against us and blocking our way. Despite the gender limitations imposed on me, the experiences intensified my longing to be away from Nodaway County: I was living in Technicolor rather than black and white.

As energized as I was by these intense experiences, I had to return to Missouri that fall. I had promised Amy that she would be able to finish high school with her class if she would take her freshman year off to go with me to Yugoslavia and, obviously, I needed to make money. The room where the English Department met on the first day of the semester airlessly pressed in on me. The same stale opinions and stodgy pedant preoccupations pulled at whatever spirit I had managed to summon for my return to the department. The department had not changed, and my life there would not change except perhaps grow more routinized and confining.

I began corresponding with a man I had met a couple of years earlier. When we ran into each other at a conference that spring, we recognized each other at once—as readers, seekers, lonely souls. We saw qualities in each other that spoke to what, somewhere deep inside us, we had always been looking for—and, along with that, uncharted territory, the possibility of a new beginning. I had a choice to make. I could risk my career, my livelihood and my emotional safety by going to another place and a second marriage, or I could stay put with all that meant.

I chose to leave and I never regretted it. That's a whole other story.

* * *

On my return trips from Maryville, I think about the place for several hours. It grabs onto me every time, pulling me back into a swirling pool of images, dark, foreboding ones of fly-covered dead carp flung on smelly backwater riverbanks by drunken fishermen and of wading children pulled into eddies in the sediment-filled Missouri. Their fathers drown with them as they try to snatch them back.

My brooding ruminations have spent themselves by the time I reach Des Moines. Surrounding me on all sides, trucks race down I-80, eighteen wheeled barges in a dredged concrete river across the Midwest. The truck drivers push relentlessly toward one ocean or the other, oblivious of the people and small towns off the road. This part of the barren, claustrophobic road trip turns me toward another point of reckoning long ago. On that solitary road trip, I descended from the mesa at the edge of Albuquerque back to fourteen years of confronting myself and the Missouri valley's impact, for good or for bad, on my character and my choices. I am taking this September road trip from the other side of those fourteen years in Maryville and now, twenty-eight years after moving away the second time. The place still has a primal attraction, but I have made peace with it, nodding in careful respect at its pitfalls and embracing the good that was there for me, too.

I turn on the radio, happy that I am in range of the NPR station in Iowa City. I repeatedly hit the search button, past country western, past HyVee grocery ads, past soft rock, and the weather until I hear Satie's "After the Rain." My brother Max played that for me on his grand piano in Los Angeles one afternoon. We sat silently together in his living room, the piano speaking for us in a language we both understood. I wish he were sitting here beside me today; I could tell him how I left Maryville not once, but twice, and that I am now on the way to integrating within myself the paradoxical place I started from and the places I traveled to, and what a trip it has been. Maybe he would tell me about his odyssey, too.

When I am almost to Iowa City, I take a cut-off skirting Cedar Rapids to Highway 151. Now that I am away from the interstate, the patchwork quilt hills painted by Grant Wood unfold ahead, serene and soothing. The landscape opens in front of the Nissan as it climbs toward the top of the big bluff right outside Dubuque. At the top of the bluff, I lean forward to catch the first sight of the Mississippi, its broad expanse gleaming below. Within ten miles of entering Wisconsin, I hit a detour diverting me to Hazel Green. I notice a road sign, "Historical Marker ½ mile" and pull off there. I pushed hard to get across Iowa, and I need to stretch and get some fresh air.

The historical marker intrigues me. This spot, the sign explains, marks the "Point of Beginning." It was here, in 1831, that surveyors crossed the Mississippi from Illinois and began to measure off the boundaries of a new state, Wisconsin. I wonder if I should put a marker there, too, for myself. Since leaving Missouri that second time, I have traveled, engineered a new career path, broken through some glass ceilings, loved, read, and grown, but it was in Wisconsin that I found solid ground.

I pull into the driveway, finally home. I see a bank of lush green lilies of the valley spreading down the slope toward the lake. Oh. Garden work. The shovelful of lilies of the valley I transplanted from my sister's yard in Missouri years ago has taken vigorous root here, and the sweet-smelling, poisonous plants now threaten to over-run the native irises at the base of the hill. It will take some spade work to bring the two back into balance.

"Welcome back. Have a good trip?" my husband asks.

"About the same as usual. How was the conference?"

"My presentation went well—about seventy-five people in the audience—and people came up afterward with some good questions. The board meeting so-so. Tedious—the usual games."

"I don't know that anyone has ever written on their gravestone 'sorry I missed the meeting.' I haven't made a presentation since retiring. I miss that, but I can't say I miss the meetings and banquet lunches."

We settle into a porch swing looking out over Lake Monona. I tell him about the ravaged land and vanquished landmarks, the dropped chances to talk, and the homestead turned manor. I rest my hand on his thigh, and we sit silently swinging with no need to say more.

The sun, a dull orange sphere patched with lavender, sinks into Lake Monona at the end of this shortened September day.

"Did you bring back some tomatoes?"

"Oh yes! My brother still had tomatoes growing in his garden. No killing frost yet. He sent some home with me. Tomato salad for dinner?"

Acknowledgments

I get by with a little help from my friends.
—The Beatles

My husband George and my friends, Jean Lind and Agate Nesaule, encouraged me to write this book every step of the way. Without their loyal support, I probably would have hit "delete" on this text a long time ago.

Jean Lind and Sandra Ihle reviewed drafts of the manuscript and gave me valuable suggestions for revising and copy editing. I appreciate the time and effort they put into making this final product better.

Remembering...

What we remember and how we remember it is a selected fiction. Lawrence Durrell wrote, "We live...lives based upon selected fictions. Our view of reality is conditioned by our position in space and time—not by our personalities as we like to think. Thus, every interpretation of reality is based upon a unique position. Two paces east or west, and the whole picture is changed." In this memoir, I've recorded pieces that are me as I remember them. Other people, even those who know me well, would come up with different versions of me in the first half of my life—based on their selected fiction.

I changed the names of several people in the book while trying to keep the integrity of the experiences intact.

About the Author

Rose Ann Findlen is a retired professor and college administrator currently living in Madison, Wisconsin. She is the author of *Missouri Star: The Life and Times of Martha Ann "Mattie" (Livingston) Lykins Bingham* (2011); *Borderland Families Always on the Edge: Journey of the Lykins, Peery, and Heiskell Families along the Missouri Kansas Border* (2011); and a book of short stories, *Waiting for the Fall* (2021).

www.ingramcontent.com/pod-product-compliance
Lightning Source LLC
Chambersburg PA
CBHW031953080426
42735CB00007B/374